CURING CORRUPTION

HOW YOU CAN SOLVE THE REAL PANDEMIC OF OUR TIME

DR BRENDA HATTINGH

Disclaimer:
None of the methods mentioned in this book and/or others,
should be undertaken without the supervision of your healthcare
professional and or physician

Cover design by Zander Hattingh
Editing by Copy-Writing: Quality Writing and Editing Services
Website: http://www.copy-writing.co.za;
Email: david.barraclough@copy-writing.co.za
Graphics by Gerhard Snyman
Website: http://www.gerart.co.za; email:
Email: info@gerart.co.za

ISBN: 9798699024643

Published by:
Currency Communications. (Pty. Ltd.)
Johannesburg. South Africa.

CURING CORRUPTION

HOW YOU CAN SOLVE THE REAL PANDEMIC OF OUR TIME

DR BRENDA HATTINGH

Published by:
Currency Communications Pty.Ltd.
Johannesburg.

This book is dedicated to everyone who is

committed to securing a positive future,

now and for generations to come.

CONTENTS

PART 4

PART 5

OoooOooo

THANK YOU

This book was written as part of a two-book series titled: *Curing Corruption*. The title of book one is, *Curing corruption. 7 Things you can do to solve the dilemma of our time.*[1]

Although the two books cover different parts of corruption and authentic living, there are some parts that overlap and might be repetitive. Fortunately, this has a positive effect, as repetition enhances memory.

It is suggested you read both books.

Thank you to all my friends and family who have encouraged and supported my work.

My appreciation goes to the publishers, Currency Communications International in Johannesburg, South Africa.

To Mark Mattson – my deepest appreciation for your editing, fine focus, insight, and attention to detail. To Gerhardt Snyman, a refined and gifted artist, my deepest thanks for the graphics.

My hope is that the information contained in this book will in some way assist and enlighten all who read these pages while inspiring you to take action to create a new, positive, and prosperous future that benefits all.

Stay safe

Brenda Hattingh
16 October 2020
Pretoria. South Africa.

PART 1

INTRODUCTION

Over the last year, we have not only experienced the challenges of the Covid-19 pandemic and subsequent lockdown, but we also experienced people taking to the streets in protesting violence, corruption, racial and gender discrimination, global warming, and other social issues.

Expectations

Expectations are that leaders and governments will solve these issues.

Unfortunately – it doesn't work that way. People are going to be disappointed.

The reason is that, after all the effort, organisation, protests, marches, upheavals, requests, petitions, and expectations – things could, and usually do, just go back to the way they were. This could leave many people angry, frustrated, disappointed – even defeated. People become fatalistic and complacent.

The question is: Why?

The answer is: Issues like corruption, violence, discrimination, and other social challenges, are not the real problem. Yes, you read correctly.

These are only symptoms of the real underlying issue, an underlying cause, to be found on a deeper, micro-level. Corruption, violence, and discrimination is an effect only.

Raising awareness

For many, the intention to stop violence and reverse corruption is valid and the motivation to make a difference is sound. However, the *methods* in addressing these issues, are mostly superficial, if not ineffective. Although these undertakings do raise awareness for these issues… the real problem as the underlying cause, is very seldom identified and resolved. These issues then remain and even escalate.

The reason is: There is another step that needs to be taken.

This brings us to the question is: How do we really solve these issues? How do we solve the real problem of corruption?

Identifying the root cause of corruption

Currently, the issue of corruption and violence - be it police violence, gender violence, family violence, criminal violence, and global corruption, is addressed through law-enforcement. Unfortunately, it doesn't solve the real issue.

As said before, these issues are only symptoms, be it very destructive symptoms at that, of the real problem rooted elsewhere. Addressing the symptoms alone is like trying to put a band-aid on a broken leg and expecting the person to walk.

The truth is: you can only solve a problem by getting to the root cause of the issue and solving the real issue. The rest will follow. This requires *out-of-the-box thinking.*

The question is: How do we solve the issue of corruption?

Einstein said:

"You cannot solve a problem with the same mindset with which it was created. You need to create a whole new mindset."

Creating a new mindset

The answer is obvious: We need a whole new mindset to identify the real, root cause of corruption. The challenge is to resolve the real issue at its micro-level. The symptoms will be resolved over time. It is like mending a broken leg with orthopaedic surgery. The pain will subside over time and the patient will be able to walk again.

There are no quick fixes.

The solution lies in doing the right things right!

The question is: What is the real underlying issue of corruption? How do we solve this issue? What is your role in this process?

In this book we will focus on answering these questions in our attempt to *cure corruption*. Ps. the same methods can be used for solving other social issues like violence, crime, and discrimination.

In this book your will find:

- The real, root-cause of corruption
- How to solve the root-cause
- Your role as part of the solution

Before we can address these three issues, it is important to start at the beginning and cover some background.

oooOooo

PART 2

BACKGROUND

Corruption as public enemy

Corruption has become one of the most rampant public enemies. Like the COVID-19 virus, it impacts everybody's lives. Those who suffer the most are mainly businesses, taxpayers and the most vulnerable in society.

Like the COVID-19 virus, corruption is invisible and has devastating consequences. The only sign of this threat is when the symptoms surface and become visible as lies, deception, destruction, stealing, money laundering, crime, violence, waste, and loss.

A country like South Africa

For example, a country like South Africa alone has lost more than ZAR 700bn to corruption over the last two decades.[2] Over the last few years these numbers have escalated and do not take recent COVID-19 corruption scandals into account.

Just as guideline, this could have paid for:

- 13 000 000 children clothed and fed for 3 years - or –
- 15 000 000 children provided with 200 000 pre-schools/day-care centres with 2 000 000 qualified

caregivers/teachers or –

- 7 000 000 school children free schooling for seven years
- 5 000 000 students for a free three-year Bachelor's degree or –
- 4 000 new or upgrading of existing schools & 5 000 clinics & 5 000 frail care centres for the elderly or –
- New houses for a whole squatter camp with 35 000 000 people
- Creating 2 000 000 new jobs[3]

The collapse of a country like South Africa has also been predicted. According to Eunomix Business and Economic Ltd., South Africa faces a precipitous economic and political collapse by 2030, unless it changes its economic model and implements growth-friendly policies.[4]

This political and economic risk consultancy forecasts that South Africa will rank near the bottom of a table of more than 180 countries in terms of security, similar to Nigeria, and Ukraine and have prosperity akin to Bangladesh or Ivory Coast.[5]

Global submission to corruption

Most people have given in to corruption. If they had taken a stand, it , not be a pandemic.

Most African and South American countries fall in the same category as above. Other countries are not far behind. It is just as relevant to the Americas, European, Eastern, and Asian countries.

Corruption is the real global pandemic of our time…and it is not being treated as other pandemics.

Corruption is a global dilemma.

Corruption in all its forms weakens the very fibre of our social structures. Unattended, our social systems begin to disintegrate ... and eventually dissolve leaving people and the economy destitute. Solving this issue should be priority number one for everyone if we intend to create a new, prosperous future and leave a flourishing society for generations to come.

Current strategies

Law enforcement and current Loss Management[6] strategies, also do not solve the issues at hand. The reason is – these interventions primarily focus on curbing the symptoms of corruption with law enforcement, without taking the real underlying cause of the problem into consideration.

Corruption, like the COVID-19 and the HIV-AIDS pandemics, needs to be addressed at the root cause and eradicated at the grass-root, micro-level. Everyone should be involved.

Complacency

However, most people are complacent, have become desensitized, and believe that corruption only refers to a criminal component in government and business structures. They feel that the government needs to 'do something' and that 'these people' need to be 'found guilty and put away'. Even some definitions referred to below, refer to corruption as the evil doings of *other people* – as outside the self.

However, corruption, includes much, much more than meets the eye.

The question is: Why are some people immune to the seductions of life while others are not?

To some or other degree, corruption applies to every single person on this planet as every person is affected in some or other way. Ignorance is not bliss!

Getting to understand what corruption is

The problem to start with is – there is no consensus on what 'corruption' means. We also find different views concerning the definition of corruption. This means that to begin with, we need to contend with confusion, misunderstanding, and uncertainty concerning both the concept and root cause of corruption. This results in incorrect and ineffective methods of addressing corruption from the start.

The first challenge is to understand corruption in its entirety and then devise ways and means of eradicating this destructive force from the fabric of society.

Current definitions of corruption

There are currently many different definitions of corruption that include:

'Corruption is dishonest or fraudulent conduct by those in power, typically involving bribery.'

Or –

'Corruption *is dishonest action that destroys people's trust in the person or group, like the news of* corruption *in how your bank is run, that makes you close your account and invest your money somewhere else.'*[7]

Or –

The process by which a word or expression is changed from its original state to one regarded as erroneous or debased.'

Or –

'Corruption is dishonest behavior by those in positions of power, such as managers or government officials.'[8]

Or –

'Corruption is the misuse of public office (by elected politicians or appointed civil servants) for private gain.'[9]

Or –

'Corruption is the misuse of entrusted *power (by virtue of heritage, education, marriage, election, or appointment) for private gain.'*[10]-

Or

Corruption is the abuse of public or private office for personal gain. It includes acts of bribery, embezzlement, nepotism, or state capture. It is often associated with and reinforced by other illegal practices, such as bid-rigging, fraud, or money laundering.'[11]

Social view of corruption

Most of the definitions above suggest that many people view corruption as a product of big business and mismanaged governments. As such, there is an assumption that these sectors bear responsibility for corruption, and thus there is no call to take personal and/or social responsibility and/or action.

However – I believe that corruption has not yet been adequately addressed and resolved because – very few people have got to the root cause of corruption.

Once we understand the fundamental cause of corruption, we can weed it out. Only when corruption is addressed at a fundamental level – can it be eradicated.

Meaning of the word 'corruption'

The word 'corruption'[12] comes from the Latin word *corruptus* made up of two parts, namely *cor* meaning 'completely' and *rumpere,* meaning 'to break'.

The word 'corruption' means to 'completely break' or 'break to pieces'; 'destroy' and 'ruin'. In its broadest sense, the fundamental meaning of corruption is:

Corruption means breaking the universal law of truth, honesty, and integrity for self-serving purposes.

This could include or exclude criminal behavior.

Corruption and breaking the law

Many forms of corruption are a criminal offence and therefore, punishable by law. Governments are trying law-enforcement to curb the pandemic of corruption.

On a higher universal level, corruption is all about breaking the one major Universal law that is: *The law of the right use of personal and collective power to the benefit of all.*

This is the law of *'The right use of your life force'.*

'Corruption is the abuse of power'.

The solution is teaching people the 'right use of power'. This calls for a whole new mindset and a whole new intelligence – Power Intelligence (PI)[13]. Power Intelligence is the intelligence of the future. We will focus more on PI later in this book,

Corruption and truth

We can also better understand a term like 'corruption' by looking at the opposite. The opposite of corruption is *honesty.*

It is all about truth.

Corruption is dishonesty – the opposite of truth, honesty, and integrity. Corruption is living the lie.

When there is honesty, truth and integrity, there also is openness, trust, transparency, and flow. Creating flow is the pinnacle of real, authentic success.[14] At this level, people, companies, organisations, and countries, flourish and grow.

Corruption is the lie that sabotages this authentic success process and renders it dysfunctional.

Corruption and real authentic success are therefore mutually exclusive.

When one rears its head, the other leaves. In a corrupt world – the delusion takes over.

Corruption as the delusion

Corrupt behavior is delusional behavior. Accompanying this delusional lie, we find fear, anxiety, and deception – especially self-deception and denial.

It becomes more and more difficult to eradicate corruption once the lie, fear, and anxiety, as parts of the ego, have taken hold. The ego-lie is a hard taskmaster who will not let go without resistance – even a fight.

Corruption also has many faces

The many faces of corruption

Although there are no 'good' synonyms for corruption, it can include concepts and faces like; dishonesty, deceit, deception, fraud, lying, cheating, infidelity, waste in all its forms, misconduct, duplicity, double-dealing, law-breaking, crime, criminality, or delinquency.

- **Different forms of corruption**

Corruption wears many faces that change from one form to another to protect the lie and deception. Lies change into deceit, change into stealing, change into crime. The challenge is to nip it in the bud.

The life of corruption depends on maintaining these faces, lies and deceptions. Sometimes deception is deployed out of ignorance or unconsciously out of self-deception and delusional thinking.

This leads to more lies, blame-shifting, excuses, the lack of transparency, and a negation of responsibility.

- **Examples of corruption**

Forms of corruption include the multinational company that pays a bribe to win the public contract to build the local highway, despite proposing a sub-standard offer.

It could be the politician redirecting public investments to his hometown rather than to the region most in need.

It could be the public official embezzling funds for school renovations to build his private villa. It could be the manager recruiting an ill-suited friend for a high-level position.

Corruption could include a marriage where the partners cheat on each other. Family members backstabbing each other, or children being corrupted by older children to lie and steal - even by adults.

At the end of the day, those hurt most by corruption are the world's weakest and most vulnerable.[15]

Children and corruption

Even this very selective view negates the fact the children stealing their classmates' cell phones; youths lying to their teachers and parents; children cheating in tests or bribing others to do their homework. Children gossiping about each other or harassing friends on social media.

These are the early breeding grounds for possible corruption on a larger scale at a later stage. The seeds of corruption are sown at an early age and can grow to lawlessness and crime.

People are desensitised

Unfortunately, by narrow margining the definition of corruption – people, especially leaders and CEO's of large companies have become desensitised and complacent where the true meaning of corruption in its widest form, is concerned.

Like one small virus created a whole epidemic - so does one small corrupt idea and act also have the potential in becoming an epidemic – even a pandemic.

However, most of the time corruption is a conscious choice that always leads to devastation. The outcome of these choices will depend on the quality of your moral fibre.

Corruption and moral fibre

We need to start at the beginning if we are serious about finding the root cause of corruption.

The beginning of corruption can be found as a fundamental untruth about:

- Who we are,
- What our purpose is,
- What authentic success really means, and
- How to create a quality lifestyle.

This leads to a lack of moral fibre. The lack of moral fibre is the lie about:

- How we can achieve success, progress, abundance, and quality living.
- It is the lie about what makes us happy.
- It is a lie about the very essence of life and living.
- It is the lie about our personal and collective power and the use of power.

The lie also includes the mindset that someone else is responsible for your suffering. This also includes that you are entitled to steal to make up for the discrepancies. This kind of mindset is fundamental to many corrupt acts today.

With the lie come uncertainty, fear, and anxiety. Corruption is a manifestation of this condition. In essence corruption is an error and incompetence that leads to captivity and imprisonment of the self and others in a make-believe world of delusion.

Corruption only gives a moment of relief of the anxiety, fear and lie. It then has to be repeated to maintain the delusion. One thing leads to another and corruption escalates.

Unless, someone takes a stand and it is topped.

Corruption and misinformation

Corruption is the result of:

- Misconception of what authentic success looks like
- An erroneous mindset of fear and lack that leads to destructive behaviour.
- A tainted, false, degrading, and/or the perverse way people view themselves, other people, life, successful living
- People not understanding what real happiness is

This error is inherent in all people. We all have the potential to revert to corrupt behaviour when under pressure.

The only difference is if and how we choose to express this corrupt part of self – or not. Corrupt behaviour can include criminal behaviour or not. Only truth and a deep understanding of reality can set us free.

Corruption and erroneous programming

At the root of all corrupt thoughts, ideas, and acts, lies erroneous mental, emotional, educational, psychological, religious, spiritual, and/or social programming.

These inner programs function much like our DNA that predisposes much of our physical and psychological functioning and even our behaviour.

How we choose to express – or not express – the underlying fear and anxiety is a matter of our level of awareness, or level of mindful living and personal and/or collective choices.

These underlying lies, fears, anxiety, and negativity lead to mental health issues.

Corruption as mental health issue

By understanding the dilemma and committing to cure corruption as COVID-19-of-the-mind, like a mental health and social, financial, cultural, leadership, government, and religious wellness issue – we can not only secure a sound foundation for the future but also leave a positive legacy for generations to come.

Corruption is mental health issue and should be treated as such.

Mental health includes our emotional, psychological, and social well-being. It affects how we think, feel, and act. It also helps determine how we handle stress, relate to others, and make choices.

Mental health is important at every stage of life, from childhood and adolescence through adulthood.[16]

Mental health disorders refer to a wide range of mental health conditions - disorders that affect your mood, thinking and behaviour. Examples of mental illness include depression, anxiety disorders, eating disorders, schizophrenia, addictive behaviours.[17]

We can see 'corruption' as symptom of this list as it includes delusions, depressions, anxiety, addictive behaviour, and erroneous thinking.

Corruption and physical health issues

On the other hand, corruption leads to physical health issues. This includes cancer, neuro-muscular disease, Alzheimer's, dementia, and other neuro-dysfunctions.

Prisoners in jail are prone to serious physical ailments. Corruption makes you physically sick. Men are prone to prostate cancer and women to breast cancer.

The reason is that the body cannot lie. An overdose of negativity, stress, addictions, obsessions and compulsions, deteriorate physical as well as mental health.

Building moral fibre

Like the COVID-19 and even the HIV-AIDS pandemics, corruption can be curbed and cured by raising awareness – by finding deeper truth in new information, education, training and the development of a new value system.

Mindfulness, consciousness, and moral fibre act as our immune system against the seductions of life.

We can mindfully, and consciously, build moral fibre – by

taking responsibility for ourselves and others. The challenge is to place the responsibility back in the hands of every person.

This is where each one of us come in. You can change the whole pandemic of corruption, just where you are. The last part of this book will show you how.

Immunizing society

Once we understand the fundamental cause of corruption – we can not only curb and cure the destructive influences. We can also immunize society against further destruction while laying a new foundation for authentic success and progress.

Social responsibility

Everyone has a role to play in the prevention of the spreading of this 'mental-virus'. The same effort put into preventing the spread of the Covid-19 virus, should be put into preventing the spread of the corruption-mindset.

Everyone has a role to play. Each person needs to accept the responsibility to curing the real pandemic of our time.

We will focus on this in more detail in part three.

Corruption is not our natural state. First, we need to focus on the truth about you, me and the whole of humanity.

The challenge is to go deep down right to a DNA level in to find answers to our questions and solutions for our dilemmas.

oooOooo

PART 3

OUR DNA SUCCESS-BLUEPRINT

The truth about humanity

All people are born with a DNA-blueprint for real, authentic success, health, wealth, and happiness found in every cell of our body.[18]

This *DNA success-blueprint* holds all the information, processes, patterns, plans, and keys to unlocking a quality life that benefits everyone. It is given to us as our real authentic potential (power-on-hold) at birth.

This means, we have a real-me, authentic self that holds the keys to everything we want and need including solutions to all and every problem and challenge we encounter during the journey of life.

The question is: If this is true (and it is) then why all the suffering, conflict, violence, and corruption? What happened that we forfeited this wonderful gift?

To answer these questions, we need to take a closer look at our DNA success-blueprint.

Our DNA success-blueprint

In every cell of our body we find a DNA-blueprint of who we really are. During the Genome Project[19], it was revealed that our DNA not only contains the blueprint for our body and physical functioning, it also contains the blueprint for our emotions, mental inclinations, and spiritual tendencies.

Our DNA-blueprint functions something like a microchip that contains all the programs we need to be healthy, wealthy, happy, and successful, while creating a flourishing, quality life, that benefits everyone.

The major questions are: If we have all the power and potential already encoded as our blueprint at our disposal, why all the crime, anger, corruption, poverty, mental health issues, and depression? What happened to all this power and potential?

The answer is: We became disconnected.

Disconnection from the universal matrix

Just like your cellular phone loses a signal and you struggle to communicate, so we lost our connection to our DNA-blueprint, our real-me authentic self and its connection to higher planes and the universal matrix.

The universal matrix is like a major universal internet system. It connects everything to everything else and hold all the information, solutions, plans and projects we need. Unfortunately, this system is dysfunctional in most people.

Today we find these disconnected parts in our DNA defined as junk-DNA.

- ## Junk DNA

Up and till now, scientists didn't know what the junk-DNA was meant to do. With the help of the research done during the Genome Project, we can now consciously and mindfully tap into this power and protential of our real-me, authentic self. From here we can tap into the universal web and create a whole new quality of life that benefits everyone.

- ## Creating the shadow ego-self

Unfortunately, during the time of the disconnection, and in place of the real-me authentic self, humanity created a synthetic self, and shadow part of self or a shadow ego-self.

It is this part of self that is corrupt.

Life is a choice. Some people choose to reflect the real-me authentic self while others choose to express the shadow ego-self in deception and corruption.

The question is: How did we become disconnected in the first place?

- ## How we became disconnected

DNA functions at its peak performance when it is connected to and aligned with the universal web and fine-tuned to the universal frequency of life. Scientists have identified this frequency as 528 Hz.

This is also the frequency of love and compassion. At any level lower than this, the DNA connections begin to frazzle until it becomes disconnected.

- **Wrong use of free-will**

Humanity became disconnected when they chose to use their free-will, as the power of choice, to further their own advantage. People started making self-serving choices that to the disadvantage of others.

They disconnected from the universal web thereby creating duality and separation. There was now a you and me. People turned on each other. Conflict emerged.

- **Ignoring universal laws**

People started negating the universal laws, including the law of *the right use of power*. They tuned in to lower, more convenient frequencies and started doing what is easy and not what is right.

The DNA success-blueprint began to frazzle and fray. Universal understanding, mindfulness, consciousness, health, wealth, and human potential was lowered

When we include contaminated food, water, pollution, and the abuse of the planet, the vibrations are lowered more rapidly. Also included are contaminated hearts and minds that create a reality of fear, crime, violence, corruption, disease, and delusion.

The only way back is to stop the downward spiral and turn the process around.

Solving the real problem

The only way we can solve the issue of corruption is to learn about the real-me authentic self and the shadow ego-self and understand what it will take to heal, connect, and restore the original DNA success-blueprint.

To understand how to restore our original DNA success-blueprint, we first need to take a closer look at the two sides of self.

By now we are aware that on the one side we all have a connected, real-me, higher, authentic self. On the other side we have a disconnected, shadow ego-self.

These two sides are constantly in conflict with each other.

The real-me authentic self

We have heard so much about the original or 'authentic self' that we are compelled to ask the following important questions.

What is the 'authentic self'? Where is it and what does it look like? Why did we lose this part of self? How do we find it and reconnect again? How do we solve our current issues, including corruption?

The book, *Coaching yourself to ultimate success. Who coaches who?*[20] contains a deeper understanding of this disconnected and forgotten part of self.

However, for now, we would like to touch on just a few essential concepts to grow in our understanding of the real-me, authentic self who holds our DNA success-blueprint.

- **What does 'authentic' mean?**

The terms 'original', 'authentic', 'real', 'higher' or 'soul' self'[21] are used interchangeably in literature. This refers to the original spiritual, light, or higher aspects of the individual self.

The 'authentic self' is the original whole, connected self, the healed self, the 'whole integrated self', or in religious terms, the Holy self. At the same time our authentic self is connected to and one with the universal cosmic web of life, higher consciousness, one-mind, or God-self.

- **Connected**

Here we connect to the awareness of our self as a unique authentic spiritual soul-person or individual.[22] On the flip side of the coin, we also find an awareness of 'authentic self' as part of the universal web, the divine universe or, 'one-song' and the Creator of creation.

- **Part of the universal matrix**

The whole of creation is created from of cosmic light and sound found on different wavelengths and different frequencies. We are therefore also a being of light and a 'note', a sound, or word of truth, in the symphony we call Creation. We were called into existence by the Creator.

Just as the song needs the notes, the notes need the song. One can only find meaningful self-expression as part of the harmony with the Oneness.

All this takes place on different wavelengths, frequencies, or 'rays of light'. Because we resonate at different levels, we attract different people, things, and situations into our life who align with our resonance.

- **Making your unique light imprint**

As a multi-dimensional spiritual light being, we have the opportunity and potential to make a personal unique light imprint on the fabric of life. By living in this conscious awareness of the power of our real-me, authentic self, we can change the world. We can even co-create miracles.

We were created to live 'happily ever after' by just being our authentic, real-me self in everything we do. This gives substance and meaning to our existence, not only in physical reality but also on higher universal/spiritual planes.[23]

This power and potential are encoded as our DNA success-blueprint. Everyone has this potential, as everyone has a DNA success-blueprint.

No-one is excluded.

Derailment

Unfortunately, we lost this ability. We became disconnected, forgot who we are, were derailed, and started living according to the programming and brainwashing from other people living on lower frequency and influences. People think this is Truth.

People became mindless while living unconscious meaningless self-destructive lives. They started living from disconnected, unsound or insane minds and created the insane illusion we call the ego-reality.

In the end, we not only forgot our authentic self, we became enslaved by the lower ego-self and all the trappings it includes. In short – we fell from grace.

The real-me authentic self

We need to answer a few questions.

Where is the authentic self? What does it look like and how do we get reconnected and remember who we are?

- **Where is the real-me authentic self now?**

The authentic self is where it has always been and will always remain – on the higher, universal, or spiritual planes.[24]

It is the true, real, original, immaculate, perfect and pure concept, the perfect blueprint or 'whole image' of the soul, held by the universal mind of Source – God.

- **What does the real-me authentic self, look like?**

As a spiritual light being, the authentic self is cosmic light[25]. Yes, each one of us has a unique light imprint, unique sound, tone, resonance, and a unique personal individual quality.

This is the same 'stuff 'the universe, including planets, the sun, galaxies, and the Milky Way are made of. Cosmic light takes on different densities, forms, and shapes.

 The only place we don't find cosmic light is in black holes. Here we find the absence of light.

➢ **Unique light imprint**

Yes, each one of us has a unique light imprint, unique sound, tone, resonance, a unique individual quality, with unique potential. Because of this, you are priceless.

On the next page we find an artist's view of the real-me authentic self. Here we find that the body is within our personal 'light bubble' that is open, honest, and uncorrupted.

> ## The **solution to corruption**

Corruption is like a black hole that sucks everything and everyone into darkness It is this part of self who can solve the corruption dilemma. This part is you!

Greater good

Although it is unique and individual it only becomes meaningful when it is expressed as part of the universal, Divine Matrix, Oneness, or in religious terms, the body of Christ. "Christ' means the *anointed* – the *anointed with Light*.

This is the whole-self, or holy self, or *anointed with light self*. Here we commit to the greater good of self and everyone else, including nature.

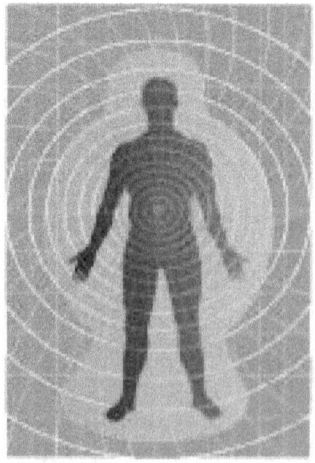

Real-me self, open and honest

The truth is that this is who we authentically are. This is where our roots should be. The challenge is to raise our awareness, develop consciousness, and live a mindful life of who we really are. This is the Truth.

Unfortunately, there is the corrupt shadow ego-self we need to contend with.

The shadow ego-self

Unfortunately, each one of us has parts of the self that have been hurt, abused, disconnected, splintered, fragmented, or 'broken off'. There are also parts we have not yet become aware of or discovered.

This means we haven't identified with, connected to, grown, developed, or evolved in these dark, shadow, fragmented areas of self. This leaves many dark-spots or blind-spots in our perception of life and living as we perceive reality through the brokenness of self.

- **Blind spots**

The unresolved issues, ignorance, and faulty ideas, and delusional programming, form *blind spots* or *black holes* in our personal space or Reticular Activating System (RAS).

This tarnishes our perception, for we see life through these issues. We project the issues on to reality and think it is the truth. We see life through tainted glasses.

The truth is, we see ourselves mirrored in the world around us. If we want to change the world – we need to start with self.

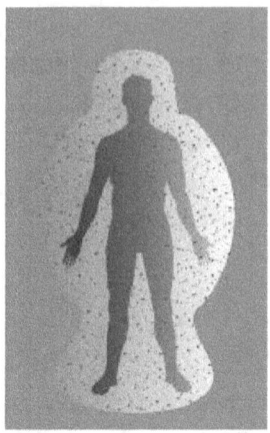

Closed shadow ego-self

Above you find an artist's view of what the shadow ego-self looks like. This is not a pretty picture and people can even be ashamed of this part of self and want to hide and/or camouflage it – and they do.

- ## Ashamed of our shadow ego-self

Most people neglect to reincorporate the fragments and learn from their shadow self. This happens mostly because we are – or unaware, or ashamed of these parts that are not 'up to standard'. We rather choose to deny and ignore their existence.

People, groups, and even cultures then create a synthetic self, a delusional self, and a make-believe reality built on false perceptions, lies, and delusions, so they can feel better about themselves.

- ## Abuse

Shadow ego-dwellers will do everything and anything to maintain this image for the shadow-ego's existence depends on it. This includes lying, stealing, all forms of abuse, attack and revenge. This drains much of people's personal power and prevents them from moving forward.

This is the root cause of corruption.

- **Understanding our shadow ego-self**

However, connecting to, understanding, and taking conscious control of the shadow ego-self is a valuable step in reclaiming our power while growing in self-master and maturity. For this, we need a new kind of power and a new kind of intelligence. Power Intelligence (PI) [26] is now emerging.

PI is becoming the intelligence of the future. We will focus on Power Intelligence a bit later in this book.

If we don't make this shift, the shadow self continues to dominate our personal dynamics while influencing the path of our lives in a negative and destructive way. This influences the people around us.

At some time or another – everyone needs to stop and take personal control and responsibility for the quality of their lives. Blaming and shaming others while negating our personal responsibility, doesn't solve the problem.

Here we erroneously think the problem is outside of the self and can be found in others. People then place responsibility on others to solve the issues of the time.

Very few people know that they have the power to solve these issues, just where they are. This is part of the delusion.

Finding the solution

Solutions start to unfold when we can face our shadow side and consciously open, expose, identify the cause, and heal our negative aspects. Then we can extend a hand to others – and not before.

In the process we become reconnected to the healed, whole, holy, original, authentic self. At the same time, our DNA success-blueprint begins to reconnect as well. We not only take back our power, we also reclaim our authentic spark of life and our authentic self. We take in our real place in life and leave a lasting imprint on the fabric of life, as a legacy.

- **Facing the shadow ego-self**

The challenge is first to become conscious of and disconnect from the delusional ego-driven self with all its lies, misconceptions, and half-truths, and distorted perceptions of who we authentically are.

We need to see the liar, the plagiarist for what it is. We need to become aware of the fear, negativity, and darkness it represents.

The challenge is to mindfully raise our awareness, change our resonance, and access new levels of consciousness while disconnecting from lower, dark, destructive frequencies, and the influence in our lives. This causes an inner dissonance – even an inner battle.

- **Winning our inner battles**

This could be a particularly challenging process for those who are totally invested in the ego lives they have created.

The shadow ego-self is a hard taskmaster and will not easily let go of its ill-gained control and power position.

The greatest battles are fought within the self. We only see the results, the effects, in our external world. So, it is no use struggling with the effects without treating the cause.

These two parts of self are constantly in conflict. Our challenge is to make a choice between living an ego-centered life or a value centered life.

These are two mutually exclusive views of life, success, and quality living. If you choose to develop one side – the other side fades away.

Corruption versus authentic success

Authentic success is all about the quality of person you are becoming on the path of life.

This way of thinking comes from the higher mind and a universal awareness.

Here success is all about expressing your real self, your authentic self as who you really are, what you have, who you are becoming, what you are achieving, and the quality of your legacy you are creating.

- **You can have it all**

This determines the quality of the imprint on the fabric of life you will leave. The truth is – you can have it all. You do not need to sacrifice, lose, or corrupt your real self in the process of acquiring possessions and possessions. We were created to have it all – it is in our DNA.[27]

- **Erroneous definition of success**

The delusional definition of success is all about acquiring positions and possessions at all costs. This kind of thinking comes from the lower shadow ego-mind.

Here it is all about accomplishments and acquiring 'stuff' while gaining acceptance in the eyes of others. This is the path of self-deception and self-corruption that leads to a life of corrupting others.

The legacy you inevitably leave is one of destruction.

- **You must choose**

The path of corruption or – the path of real, authentic success is a conscious choice. You cannot have real success and corruption simultaneously side by side and expect to flourish.

Ignoring, fighting, and/or resisting corruption are ineffective strategies. The reason is, what you resist – persists.

It is like trying to stop a tsunami with a garden hose. The reason can be found in a quote from Einstein who said:

"You cannot solve a problem with the same mindset that created it. You first need to change your mindset."

To solve the issue of corruption, we first need to create a new and positive vision of the future. People need to learn what authentic success looks like.

Authentic leadership

I would like to define *an authentic leader as some-one who knows the way, goes the way and shows the way to authentic self-expression and a quality life encoded as our DNA success-blueprint.*

This so calls for a new quality of leader and leadership influence. Without this new vision, 'anti-corruption' projects are meaningless. The reason is, it is more powerful to stand for something positive than resisting and opposing the negative.

Current leaders do not necessarily have this quality and will need to make way for a new wave of quality leaders, as quantum leaders[28], who have developed New Leadership DNA.[29]

Authentic leaders understand the power of honesty, truth, and inte.grity. They are the way-showers into a new future of success and progress that benefits all.

The time has now come to heal corruption as it sabotages the real success progress by developing real, authentic leaders who have already conquered their egos.

Ego-centered versus value-centered living/leading

The summary below indicates of one of the two paths we could follow. Seven steps correspond to the seven levels of development outlined in New Success DNA.[30]

Here you will find all the necessary tools and skills to change your life to the resonance of love, light, power, wisdom, and abundance.

When we once again look at all the masters from all religions, we find that they are totally identified with their higher, authentic, soul, spiritual self.

They became one with their inner light authentic self or personal Christ self or enlightened self.

VALUE-CENTERED	EGO-CENTERED
Self-aware	Self-conscious
Self-worth	Self-centered
Self-esteem	Self-importance
Self-care	Self-serving
Self-confidence	Self-delusion
Self-respect	Self-indulgence
Self-mastery	Self-destructive

Value-centred versus ego-centred living

Above you find a summary of the soul- or value-centred versus an ego-centred approaches to life.

As exercise: Take the examples of current and past leaders like Nelson Mandela, Barak Obama, Donald Trump, Putin, Jacob Zuma, or Cyril Ramaphosa, and ask yourself which path they chose by using the table as a map. Also use it to identify where you currently are.

Corruption and Power Intelligence

Corruption is the conscious and/or unconscious sabotage of authentic success processes that benefits all people.

Corruption is the mindless use or abuse (absence-of-use) of power in all its forms. The challenge is to understand success, power, and potential. In essence, we need to develop our Power Intelligence[31] or PI.

- **Power Intelligence**

Power Intelligence is *the conscious ability to manage power and potential to the benefit of all*. Power Intelligence is the next level of human intelligence to emerge and is rapidly becoming the intelligence of the future. This calls for new leaders to step up and step forward as new pathfinders and way-showers. These are not only honest and authentic people they are also power intelligent.[32]

- **Developing Power Intelligence**

When you develop your Power Intelligence, you become mindful of your personal and universal power. You align with universal power and abide by its its laws as outlined in the book *Curing Corruption*.[33] The solution lies in committing to honesty, truth, and integrity, and securing a path of authentic success.

Here you commit to the *right use of power*.

Call for new authentic leaders

As said, corruption can be viewed as *'living the lie'*. How this lie was obtained, be it through inappropriate, ineffective, or erroneous education, training, and development; lack of moral development; false belief systems and deception; cultural, political, religious, social, or tribal brainwashing – is immaterial. The outcome is the same – destruction and suffering.

This can be changed by reclaiming your power, improving education, elevating moral development, challenging outworn belief systems, while creating a new vision of success and progress.

Corruption is mindless living, lack of awareness, negativity, disconnection, discord, and ignorance and is driven by fear. In essence, corruption is the lie and the cause of fear. We can resolve ignorance and alleviate fear. We can reverse the process, thereby curing corruption – if we know how.

This calls for a new kind of human being and a new quality of leadership. We now need authentic leaders to stand up and take in their place.

Because they have already walked the path, these people are ready and willing to heal corruption – the real pandemic of our time.

ooo0ooo

Part 4

HEALING CORRUPTION

Introduction

In the film *Forrest Gump*, with Tom Hanks in the title role, we find this inspiring man, who at the surface seems to be mentally handicapped, achieve the most extraordinary feats. He finds his happiness in his life-long love, Jenny.

However, it is the seventies and Jenny was part of the Hippy, drug, and sex-culture of the times. Jenny dies from an 'unknown' virus and Forrest is left with memories of love, fulfillment, and happiness . . . and a son. Forest jr. is healthy, happy, and very bright, and we learn – 'life is a box of chocolates'.

During the sixties and seventies, many involved in the gay and hippy cultures contracted this then-unknown virus. During these times people were caught unawares and they paid for their ignorance with their lives.

Today we know about the HIV-AIDS. Millions of people have suffered and died from HIV-AIDS and much has been done to raise awareness and provide a cure. Today, people can be immunized against HIV-AIDS.

The COVID-19 pandemic

Nearly five decades later, another pandemic erupts and cripples the world. The year 2020 will be marked in history as the year of the COVID-19 pandemic. The virus became humanity's number one threat.

Lockdown, social distancing, job losses, crippled economies, and the search for an anti-virus drug, all mark this time spent in isolation. New laws and national strategies were put into place to curb the pandemic. Everyone took responsibility and worked together to protect their own health and the health of others.

Governments, countries, and organizations, all started working together with one goal in mind that is to prevent the spread of the virus and secure the health of the people.

This brought division: One group wants to secure the health of the people while others want to secure the growth of the economy. The challenge was and still is, to find a midway between securing public safety while still growing the economy.

This calls for a new kind of leader to emerge – a real authentic leader.

The global community is united in curbing and curing the crippling attack of an unseen foe – we call a virus.

Corruption should be treated in the same manner.

There is much to learn from the processes of the HIV-AIDS campaign and the COVID-19 pandemic.

The questions are:

- What is a virus and what does it do?
- Is there a HIV-Aids or Covid-19 virus of the mind?

- What do we need to be aware of to prevent being caught unaware and even pay for our ignorance with our lives?
- How do we cure the pandemic of corruption?

Lessons from virus infections

Viruses are about 100 times smaller than bacteria and found in almost every ecosystem on Earth.[34] We find destructive viruses that cause disease and death.

We also find constructive viruses that are conducive to our health and wellbeing,

The questions are: What is a virus and how does it function? Is there something like a 'corruption virus'? What can we learn from virus infections and corruption?

- ## What is a virus?

We have a double helix DNA[35] string that holds the original blueprint of optimum functioning of who we are as a unique human being, in every cell of our body.

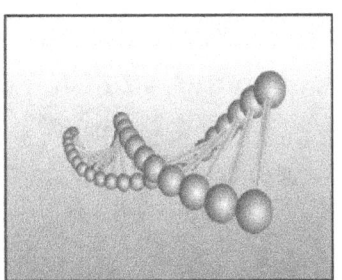

DNA with chromosomes

A virus is just one part of a DNA string known as RNA.

Where DNA can function in every cell, RNA needs a 'host' to connect to. It connects to functioning DNA and renders it dysfunctional.

A virus brings the 'lie' or disinformation, into a system.

- ## **Becoming infected**

When the virus enters a host cell it connects its disinformation package to the DNA as the information system of the host. The disinformation of the virus takes over the DNA of the host and deactivates the host's DNA and impairs normal functioning.[36] The host is now infected.

This infection renders the host powerless, it becomes dysfunctional, and can even die if not treated.

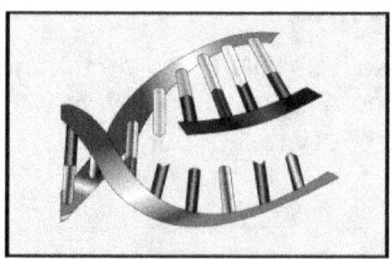

Virus connecting with DNA of host

So, a virus is an 'infectious agent'. It is a tiny information program or package, a little piece of disinformation, present in the form of genes on an RNA string.

Here we find the real cause of the dilemma we call corruption. Here we also find the answer to our social problems as solutions to social dilemmas such as violence, crime, poverty, disease, and conflict.

- ## Disinformation

Just think, one little piece of disinformation – one little lie – one false perception – one false value, disconnects one tiny functioning part of the real authentic DNA success-blueprint.

In the case of HIV-AIDS or Covid-19 infection, the immune system is disconnected resulting in global pandemics. This tiny 'lie' or corrupt particle causes disease, disintegration, decay, and if not treated – death.

As said, corruption, gender violence, discrimination, and other social dilemmas are the result or symptoms of this process.

We also find 'viruses' as disinformation, in our information systems and social media.

- ## Computer viruses

Computer viruses function in the same way as physical viruses. For example, false information gains access to our computers as a 'computer virus' and renders the programs ineffective. Information systems then become dysfunctional, crash, and can even disintegrate. The disinformation is further spread on social media.

Groups, companies, organizations, governments, and countries, – the whole of humanity – function in the same way as one interconnected, whole, fully functional living system.

If one part is infected, it renders the whole system dysfunctional. The flipside is also true. If one part is healed, connected, and become functional – it influences the whole system in the same way.

This is where our task lies. It takes but one person to stand up and change the whole system.

The reason is – we are interconnected. You can make the changes humanity now needs. In the lst part of this book we will show you how.

- **Interconnectedness**

Universally, everything is connected to everything and everybody else. Here we find everything fully functional.

One little piece of disinformation, erroneous programming, corrupt values or lie, infects and influences everything and everyone –without you even knowing the consequences.

This causes people, groups, companies, organizations, governments, and countries to become dysfunctional. If the problem is not adequately addressed at a grass-root level, it leads to deterioration and in the end destruction.

If we are unaware, in denial, or neglect to take the necessary precautions, we remain vulnerable. The pandemic spreads

The question is: Do the lessons we learn from physical and computer viruses also apply to our mental and emotional well-being?

The answer is – yes!

Human value systems

There is contaminated information, or disinformation, that, like virus programs, negatively affect human values, emotions, beliefs, and thought processes. These erroneous beliefs are not only transferred from one person to another but are also transferred from one generation to another.

It is this kind of 'infection' as disinformation, lies, ignorance, erroneous value systems and lack of understanding, inadequate moral development, ignorance and/or denial, that disables authentic functioning and causes corrupt behavior. The corrupt behavior plays out on different paying fields of life – including the economy.

Destruction is inevitable if not curbed and cured.

The question is: How do we solve the dilemma of corruption?

The challenge is to raise public awareness, transform mindsets, redevelop new education systems, and elevate belief, value and spiritual systems to a whole new level.

Steps in curing corruption

Here are a few steps we can take to cure the real pandemic of our time.

- **Getting to the root of the problem**

As said before, destructive mental 'virus programs', could gain access and render us ineffective. People become physically, mentally, emotionally, and universally/ spiritually dysfunctional. We can even lose our soul.

This is accomplished by disabling the initial connection to the authentic program, our authentic self – the DNA success-blueprint of life.

Corruption is a mental health issue that needs to be treated and healed.

- **Immunizing**

By closing and protecting systems (like computer virus protection) and immunizing people, groups, companies, and organizations against any intrusions – corruption will die a certain death - just like an isolated virus cannot survive on its own.

This could sound like a very lofty idea and unrealistic idealistic statement but … just as ways and means were found to address the HIV-AIDS and the COVID-19 pandemics – there are realistic, practical ways and means to cure corruption as a mental health issue.

It can be treated like HIV-AIDS-of-the-mind. It should get the same attention and treatment as the COVID-19 pandemic.

It will help us to understand how viruses spread.

- **Preventing the spread of viruses**

Viruses spread in many different ways.

➢ **The spread of physical viruses**

Some physical viruses are spread by insects and animals. Viruses such as influenza are spread through the air by people when they cough or sneeze. Others are transmitted by contaminated hands, food, water or direct contact.

The human immunodeficiency virus, HIV, is one of several major viruses that are transmitted during sex.

➢ **Protection against computer viruses**

Computer viruses are spread by giving a corrupt program access to your computer. Developing anti-virus programs, spy-ware, and building firewalls is a multibillion-dollar business.

This is all necessary to protect your information.

➤ **Human information systems**

Where the human information system is concerned, disinformation can also spread in different ways. With our social media, the spread is sometimes instant,

Information is processed in the brain. This is the first line we can 'firewall'. However, our real success program is part of our DNA-blueprint. Here we are connected by different frequencies.

If the information is corrupt and the frequency falls below a certain range – the DNA success-blueprint disconnects leaving people lost and helpless.

Some people think this is the way life is. Others blame the distortion on others. Few accept personal responsibility to set things right. You can be one of these few to stand up and make a difference.

If a person, company, organization, and/or country are not mentally strong, emotionally mature, or lack the right information processing strategies and discernment, they could easily fall prey to lies, deceit, and disinformation that is globally available.

The call should be for honesty, truth, integrity, and transparency. This calls for a raising of awareness to what we are exposed to, taught, what we are made to believe, and to what information people and especially children, are exposed to.

The challenge is to consciously develop this higher and new level of maturity. People need to 'grow up'.

We also need to build up immunity.

- **Viruses and immunity**

Usually. viruses are eliminated by the immune system, conferring lifetime immunity to the host for that specific virus.[37]

However, the problem with the HIV-AIDS and COVID-19 viruses is that they disconnect the genetic material responsible for our immune system and render the protective function of the immune system ineffective.

People get sick.

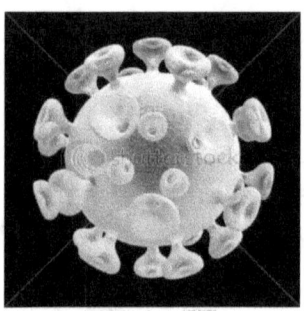

Covid-19 virus

The virus shortcuts the flow of the initial information and the body loses its power to fulfill its real authentic function. The physical body is then powerless to protect itself and becomes vulnerable to other infections.

Once the HIV leads to AIDS, as the total breakdown of the immune system, there is very little one can do except to treat the symptoms. The COVID-19 virus causes respiratory problems and can lead to death if left untreated, especially to vulnerable groups.[38]

Those who are especially vulnerable, are the sick, aged, and small children who have a low level of immunity. Building our immunity is one of our greatest challenges today. This includes physical, mental, emotional, and universal immunity.

Computer viruses and the corruption of the human mind and social systems, function in the same way. Disintegration and death are the results of untreated infections

The call is to 'immunize' people and systems. We even need to 'fire-wall' processes and people to keep them free from contamination.

For this, we need a new way of thinking and a new quality of leader – a real authentic leader.[39] These are people who are informed, fearless, and are not afraid to take a stand for what is right. They stand up, not only for themselves, but also for the greater good of humanity and generations to come.

However, we need to be informed about trojan horses.

- **Become aware of 'Trojan horses'**

'Trojan horses', phishing, or other forms of camouflage are used to gain entrance to our computers, our information and cause the damage they were created for.

The purpose is the disruption of the flow of information. It costs time, effort, and money to regain entry to the affected computer and restore the flow of information. Computer viruses have become a large concern in the information technology industry over the last decade.

In the picture below we find the invader's corrupt information program, depicted as dark, black, thought-forms. It blocks the line of information flow of the original program, and the system shuts down.

Many computers and large computer systems have crashed (and died) before computer antivirus programs became freely available.

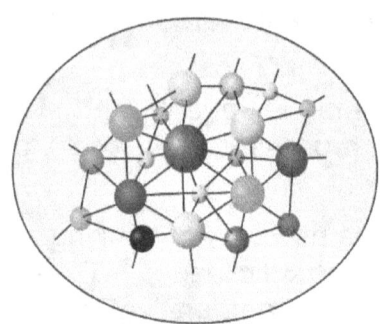

Dark invasion of the natural flow

Today we cannot think of purchasing a computer without purchasing an anti-virus program. Providing anti-virus programs has become one of the largest money-making businesses currently online.

The same applies to people.

- **Be aware of corrupt people and corrupt groups**

Corrupt people try to corrupt others in like manner. People and groups with camouflaged corrupt ideas, plans, motives, agendas, and programs, enter the lives of the unsuspecting, even gullible masses.

They create groups, clans, and even political parties you can belong to. They leave a trail of lies, deceit, deceptions, false expectations, delusional promises, and cover-ups. This causes dark destructive blockages in the natural, normal flow – the essence of success. This is destruction in the making.

Today, no informed person in their 'right mind' would use a computer to download from the internet without making sure that a computer anti-virus program has been installed and is up to date. In like manner no-one in their 'right mind' will have unprotected sex with a stranger. In the same way, no one in their 'right mind' will engage in, implement, and/or support corruption, corrupt groups, policies, values, agendas, plans, and processes.

It would be insane![40]

However, the truth is – it is happening and escalating at this moment. Corruption is therefore not, in essence, a financial and/or legal issue, but a mind-wellness issue.

Corruption and mind-wellness

We have two points of departure. On the one hand, we have healthy people, functioning from our 'right mind', sound mind or 'sanity'.

On the other hand, we have a dysfunctional situation with people operating from the disconnected 'wrong mind', unsound mind, 'insanity', or insane mind.

The disconnected unsound, 'insane' mind and corrupt ideas leave people and organizations vulnerable to the corruption, pandemic.

The questions that arise are: What is our 'right mind' and how does it protect us against corrupt mind-virus infections.

Mindful 'right mind' versus mindless 'insanity'.

The answers to these questions are easy: This 'right mind' refers to the connection with the universal mind, the universal web as our cosmic internet.

From a religious perspective, we are connected to the God-mind and Holy Spirit. Here we are connected at a deep DNA level to the Mind of the universe.

This connects us to the universal truth about who we are as authentic human beings and what life, success, progress, and happiness are all about.

Right-minded people are now awakening and taking responsibility to connect to their own DNA success-blueprint. They are then equipped to help others to do the same.

This is our responsibility in curing corruption while laying a new foundation for healthy living for generations to come.

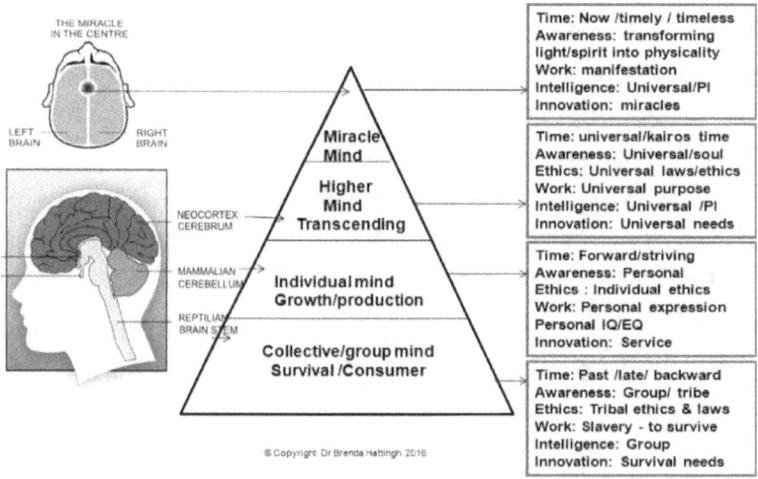

Levels of connections –levels of thinking

We gain access to this information through an open, honest approach to life and living. This is our 'right mind'. We are connected to our 'right mind', our 'sound mind' or universal consciousness, via different levels of neuro-functioning as seen depicted above.

- **Our 'right mind'**

'Right mind' refers to higher levels of consciousness and awareness, the connection with higher intelligence, our higher real-me, authentic self, universal mind, or Source.

Here we are aware, can discern right from wrong, and can detect or pick-up on negativity, lies, deception, destruction, and negativity.

This high level of awareness keeps us alert, in control, and guides us through difficult situations. Once we are connected to this level and mindfully access this frequency, we become immune to any other lower-order influences and connections.

It takes a lot of will power and self-control to stay at this level. Self-coaching is now one of the most important tools in our toolbox.

- **Being aware of lies**

With heightened awareness, we can consciously protect ourselves against unnecessary exposure to any of the lower-order information as lies, deceptions, and the bearers of corrupt, erroneous information.

People become sensitive to the lie.

Our conscience becomes highly sensitive, and we even begin to 'think with our hearts'.

This is very different to the unsound mind of corruption.

Curing Corruption

As said, corruption is a mental and emotional wellness issue playing out on the playing fields of life that include business, politics, religion, social and personal contexts.

It is possible to heal these disconnections and become immune to lies and deceit. We can consciously deny any access to dark, negative, and corrupt influences, from self, other people, circumstances, or substances that could jeopardize our emotional, mental, or spiritual connections, wellbeing, and functioning.

• Maintaining your healed mind

As long as we stay mindful, we can maintain our healed mind, secure our sanity, our functionality and ability to co-create with universal processes. By growing in conscious awareness, we will remain standing under all and every challenge we may encounter on earth.

Many leaders like Gandhi, Nelson Mandela, Martin Luther King, and others, have paved the way for us.

From a religious perspective we find grand masters like Buddha and Jesus Christ who have shown the way to this enlightened way of being.

• Rising above circumstances

Like them, we know and understand we can and should rise above destructive circumstances. We can consciously raise our frequency and we can and should become immune to corruption and the seductions of life.

We only need to stay connected and functional as we should – as our authentic self, as a light bearer, pathfinder, mapmaker, and trendsetter.

For this, we need new to upgrade our manual and toolbox of life by developing new skills and tools. How this can be achieved, including all the necessary skills and tools we will need, is outlined in the book *Power Tools for Power People*.[41]

As said, we also need to identify the many faces of the lie/disinformation.

The lie has many faces

The lie, coming from corrupt sources and ego-driven disconnected persons or groups on lower order, dark and corrupt levels of disinformation, is packaged in different forms and has different faces.

• Misinformation

These people consciously or unconsciously spread the misinformation, the lie, through their erroneous interpretations, teachings, values, beliefs, guidance, and influence.

We can directly or indirectly be exposed to the lie and erroneous teachings. How we react will all depend on how aware, mindful, and equipped we are.

• Lies are handed down

The lie can be handed down from generation to generation. This means the mind-virus is not only contagious but also 'hereditary'. Once the mind-virus takes hold, it becomes a long and arduous struggle to survive.

If you are not equipped with the correct tools and skills i.e. the truth, the loss of authentic living, or death, is inevitable.

- **The lie about who you are**

The lie is any falsehood, untruth, or half-truth about who you are, where you come from, what your purpose is, and how you should function. It takes on many forms and faces.

Most of all, the lie disregards the truth of universal cosmic truth, compassion, love, abundance, health, wealth, happiness, fulfillment of heart and soul, and the ability to co-create with Source to the benefit of all.

The lie negates the truth about your real identity as a universal/spiritual light being with a physical body, heart, mind, soul, and spirit.

The lie denies your true heritage and disconnects you from your authentic, functional higher self, your spirit, and your soul.

- **The lie steals your soul**

The lie deactivates or 'steals' your soul. It takes control, renders you powerless, dysfunctional, mindless and even useless.[42] You feel lost, helpless, alone, worthless, and afraid while living a meaningless life of constant survival from day-to-day.

You become a captive of fear.

- ## The shadow ego-lie

The lie represents the false image of the earthly ego and wants you to identify with this corrupt illusion. The lie disconnects you from your true identity and places a synthetic image in its place. The shadow ego-self has little or no conscience

Not only does the lie steal your soul and identity, it wants to keep you mindless and 'insane' meaning 'with an unsound mind'. It keeps you dependent, places you in bondage, and holds you captive to lower frequencies and the destructive, corrupt, ego teachings and destructive programming of groups, cultures, and religions of the world.

- ## The competitive ego-self

The lie introduces a false ego-self and places it in competition with the authentic soul, value-self. The lie spreads false interpretations, confusion, dissonance, darkness, false notes, fear, disintegration, and in the end, death.

The lie clouds our thoughts rendering them dysfunctional while our heart, mind, soul, and spirit, are disconnected from the frequency of truth, wisdom, love, and compassion – the frequency of miracles and true success.

Competition, struggle, resistance, and survival take the place of health, wealth, happiness, and quality living.

We lose the ability to love and be loved. This leads to a hellish kind of life. Our challenge is to hit the reset button and go back to our roots. It is time to re-root and re-boot.

Summary

Up and till now we have been looking at ways and means to curing corruption. We have in general, covered various steps that need to be considered when addressing this issue.

However, the title of this this book is; *Curing Corruption. How you can solve the real pandemic of our time.*

It is now time to get more personal and ask: How can you, just where you are, solve a global dilemma like corruption?

ooo0ooo

PART 5

HOW YOU CAN SOLVE CORRUPTION

The influence of our thoughts on DNA

Bruce Lipton's book, *The Biology of belief*[43] illustrates how our thoughts have profound effects on our behaviour and our genetic material, our genes – our DNA.

This, however, only occurs when our thought patterns are in harmony with subconscious programming, our soul, spirit, and the universal matrix.

- ### The subconscious mind

Lipton explains how the subconscious mind and the conscious mind operate independently. The subconscious mind repeatedly goes over the same behavioural responses from life.

We respond to situations stored in our subconscious, which Lipton says is, "millions of times more powerful than the conscious mind".

- ### The influence on our genes

He further elaborates by stating: "*genes are shaped, guided, and tailored by environmental learning experiences.*"

71

His theory states that we are not only the result of our genetic makeup, but rather from the influence of the environment – starting of course with our parents, teachers, leaders, and the society we live in.

This means our circumstances influence our genetic make-up. We can also influence our genetic make-up and that of others. This is called *Epigenetics.*

Epigenetics

Epigenetics is the study of how your behaviour and environment can cause changes that affect the way your genes work. Unlike genetic changes, epigenetic change is reversible. It does not change your DNA sequence, but it can change how your body reads a DNA sequence and how it is expressed.[44]

In short, Epigenetics is the study of the influence of the environment on the functioning of our genetic material or DNA. It also includes the influence of our genetic functioning on the environment.

We now learn that we are not necessarily the result of our genetic hereditary. We can also change our genetic functioning by changing our environment. Most of all we can change our genetic material, and that of others, by accessing and changing our mind and subconscious programming.

This is where one person has the power to change the world. You have the power to solve the issue of corruption.

The question is: How can one person change a global pandemic like corruption that includes other issues like, discrimination, gender violence, crime, and poverty?

• The influence of your subconscious mind

We can use a school of fish as an example of the ability that one person has to change a group, even the world.

The communication between each member of a school of fish takes place on a fundamental, electromagnetic level.

Each fish communicates subconsciously with all the other fishes in the school. The school of fish then functions as one unified whole. Just as our body functions as one unified whole.

A school of fish communicating on a genetic level

However, if one fish should change and elevate its frequency to a new higher level, it reverberates throughout the whole school of fish on an electromagnetic DNA level.

If it is beneficial to the whole school of fish, the school will change for the better. These changes could be permanent if it changes the DNA-sequencing. This is natures way of securing the best potential.

We can even identify subspecies of fish that have gone through this transformation process. They have their own genetic barcode that distinguishes them from the original group or school of fish.

- **Genetic barcoding[45]**

A barcode is an image consisting of a series of parallel black and white lines that, when scanned, relays information about a product. Barcodes are read by special optical scanners.

  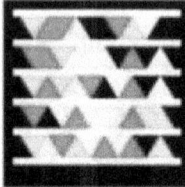

Types of general barcoding

However, we find the same processes present in living material that has a DNA-sequence as a barcode.

DNA barcoding was first introduced by Herbert[46] who is best known for his discovery and proliferation of DNA barcoding, which uses a specific section of genetic code to identify any species. This includes human DNA barcoding.

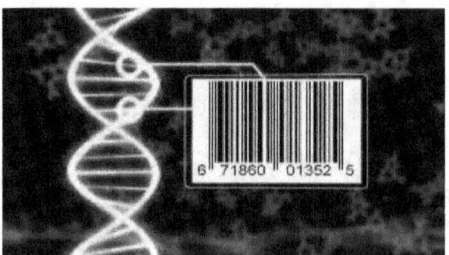

The genetic barcode

Conscious parenting

Lipton gives practical advice on 'conscious parenting' and believes that the best growth promoter for children is unconditional love. Our parents act as genetic engineers, months before conception.

All is encoded into our 'master cell'.[47]

When we have a destructive thought or emotional pattern accessing our 'master cell', we can expect the same results we find with the HIV-AIDS or CVID-19 viruses

Destructive patterns and junk genes

.Not only do these negative thought forms and feelings invade our body and mind, our light bodies - our spirit and soul are also invaded. Our higher, universal connections are rendered ineffective.

We then find dysfunctional or 'junk genes'.

The challenge is to reclaim and mine our lost potential from these junk genes.[48] All negativity, or low energy frequencies, have the ability to disconnect us from higher frequencies, higher thoughts, the higher mind or the heart[49] of source – God.

One question remains; What must we do?

In short – we need to reclaim our power, take back our authentic self, ignite quality living, heal the destructive legacy, and reactivate our multidimensional DNA.[50]

Let us start with how to heal our DNA.

Healing the mind – healing your DNA

You heal the self and connect to the higher mind by accessing higher frequencies of information, truth, and universal wisdom.

Many times, you first need to detox from toxic influences and people while unlearning lower order information to make place for a new mindset and a new lifestyle.

First you have to let go of the old.

- **Dying to the old**

Dying to the old is not always easy or painless. This can be done by exposing yourself to new information and higher truths.

It helps to find competent authentic people who can assist, help, teach, and coach you along the way.

If not, you need to do it on your own.

There is a multitude of methods you can use to heal your mind and your DNA. You will find this background information in the books. *New Success DNA*, *Power Intelligence, New Leadership DNA*, and other relevant books.[51]

You can also enroll in a personal coaching course or one of our other courses that are constantly being made available by the Centre for Power Intelligence.

For our purpose here, we will only focus shortly on a few other options.

- **Medical and psychological attention**

When a person is infected with a biological virus like HIV-AIDS or COVID-19, people immediately seek medical attention. The same attention is necessary for corruption.

- **Symptoms of a 'mind-virus'**

Although the virus-of-the-mind (mind-virus) infection, takes place on a mental-psychological-spiritual level, the same care should apply.

The physical symptom of a 'mind-virus' is 'burnout' and disintegration. This includes all the psychosomatic symptoms that accompany mental, emotional, physical, and spiritual stress and fatigue.

In essence, the body rebels against 'overuse' or 'abuse' in a mindless, plastic lifestyle of struggle and survival.

Using the brute force of personal ego driven willpower to survive, is unnatural and causes stress and further burnout. We are created to create success with effortless ease by increasing flow.

- **Burn-out**

The physical body is too fragile to withstand long periods of abuse, stress and inevitably 'burns out'. This means that many people, including many leaders in influential positions, are burnt out and depleted. The abuse of alcohol, painkillers, over-eating, drinking, partying, overspending overindulgence, and imbalance – causing addictions, obsessions, and compulsions – form part of this scenario.

When in this state, it becomes much easier to do something corrupt.

- **Dysfunctional lifestyle**

This can lead to overwork or dysfunctional work ethic, lethargy, or hyperactivity, depression, aggression, and disintegration of personal and collective systems and structures. Stress, anxiety, and fear also raise the possibility of making bad even, corrupt choices.

Medical attention should be given to the physical manifestations and all illnesses treated appropriately. These are however only the symptoms and not the original cause.

The underlying emotional dynamics, disconnections, and psychosomatic dysfunction need to be attended to as well. People can also make use of therapists, coaches, and other professional psychological and mental-health services available, to address these issues.

Prevention is also better than cure.

- **Coaching, mentoring, and education.**

Awakening individuals, teams, companies, and organisations, are now finding professional, personal, life, leadership, and/or organizational coaches who are competent in quantum coaching and the healed mind approach.

There a select few coaches and consultants who are masters in accessing, utilizing, and healing the DNA success-blueprint.

- **Coaching and mentoring**

These coaches and mentors are persons who have already excelled beyond primary, secondary, and tertiary education. They already function on the level of quaternary[52] education by utilizing the fourth dimension of connection and thinking.

The challenge is to find someone who you are confident will bring you a deeper understanding of truth and who will help you to find your truth and authentic self.

Choose someone who will help you heal the hurt, open the mind, and reclaim your DNA success-blueprint.

- **Authentic leaders, coaches, and mentors**

Remember, there are many people now using the word 'authentic' to promote their services. Many are ego-driven. Check if they use accessing and utilizing your DNA success-blueprint as part of their services.

If not – it's not really authentic.

- **Training authentic leaders and coaches**

Unfortunately, very few professional coaches, mentors and/or psychologists are currently trained in conscious DNA healing and activation.[53]

We need to train authentic leaders and coaches. If you cannot find and fit for your needs, you will need to learn to coach yourself.

However, in the end, we all personally but also collectively need to help and cure the self. This is what maturity is all about. This also has an influence on our education system.

- **Teachers, education, and education systems**

This also shines a light on the quality of teachers and the training of teachers. Developing teachers who are able to bring a healing influence to their learners by just being their authentic self, is one of our greatest challenges.

Developing a next level of education system that takes quantum thinking and quaternary education seriously, will be our next global challenge.

- **Self-healing and self-mentoring**

You can start your own self-healing and mentoring processes by becoming conscious and aware of who you are and what you want out of life. Take all the steps and requirements you need to become fulfilled, happy, and successful.

See the book *Coaching yourself to ultimate success* that includes avaible on Amazon.com. There is also a course available through Power Intelligence Leadership Academy, titled, *Coaching yourself to ultimate success.*[54]

Embark on a new adventure by attending workshops, reading new books, listening to new music and messages, while developing a new exercise and eating program. Do whatever it takes to heal your mind, your DNA, and your life.

- **Stem cell therapy**

Currently, there are various methods to heal your body, mind, heart, and soul – even your DNA.

This can include the use of sound, light and also stem cell therapy. It is of course important to understand that all interventions have a positive and negative, light, and dark side and must always be entered into with clarity and discernment.

However, we can now also add to this growing list, the use of electromagnetic therapy.

- **Electromagnetic therapy and healing DNA**

Science has established that electrical and magnetic energy exists in the human body. Some devices commonly used in mainstream medicine include the electroencephalogram (EEG) to measure electrical activity in the brain and the electrocardiogram (EKG) which measures the electrical patterns of heartbeats.

The use of electro-energy to stimulate the heart when its rhythm is disrupted is known as defibrillation. Other devices such as magnetic resonance imaging (MRI) and trans-cutaneous electrical nerve stimulation units are also used in mainstream medicine.

- **Electromagnetic energy**

Electromagnetic therapy involves the use of electromagnetic energy to diagnose or treat disease. Alternative medicine providers may offer low-voltage electricity, magnetic fields, radio waves, or other types of electromagnetic energy generated by electric currents for this purpose.

Electromagnetic energy includes electricity, microwaves, radio waves, ionizing radiation, and infrared rays, as well as electrically generated magnetic fields. Light is also a form of electromagnetic energy as previously discussed.

- **Electromagnetic devices**

In contrast to the wide range of electromagnetic energy methods that have been proven for standard medical treatment, many of the alternative electronic devices promoted to cure disease have not been scientifically proven to be effective. Most of these devices claim to offer radio waves, electrical currents, or magnetic fields.

- **Electromagnetic therapists**

In general, practitioners of electromagnetic therapy all agree that when electromagnetic frequencies or energy fields within the body go out of balance, disease and illness occur.

These imbalances disrupt the body's chemical makeup. By applying electromagnetic energy from outside the body, usually with electronic devices, it is possible to correct the imbalances in the body.

Practitioners claim that these methods can treat ulcers, headaches, burns, chronic pain, nerve disorders, spinal cord injuries, diabetes, gum infections, asthma, bronchitis, arthritis, cerebral palsy, heart disease, and cancer.

Warning: None of these therapies should be undertaken without supervision from your health-care professional and/or your physician.

- **Research**

This research is currently part of standard medical intervention.[55] We can expect it to expand and include emotional, mental, psychological, and spiritual healing as well.

As our understanding and technology develop, we can expect new methods of healing our DNA to emerge.

Artificial intelligence[56] (AI) and Nanotechnology[57] are already on the foreground.

- **Healing frequencies**

Different frequencies activate and stimulate different parts of the physical and light bodies. Some of the frequencies we need to become aware of include the following:

Activates:	Frequency
Love/compassion	528 Hz
Pineal gland	936 Hz
Intuition	741 Hz
Light centers	432 Hz

Frequencies of different aspects of self

However, DNA healing and activation is nothing new. It has been part of ancient spiritual practices for millennia. DNA healing is in essence spiritual healing – a reconnection with the universal mind, the 'right mind', or sound mind.

Universal/Spiritual DNA healing

Spiritual DNA activation in its currently available form can be traced back to over 2500 years ago and is therefore not viewed as a new phenomenon.

- **Ancient teachings**

The technique was originally performed in the Great Pyramid of Giza to prepare priests, priestesses, oracles, prophets, and high healers, for positions of power and responsibility within their communities. These were the 'worthy ones' who knew all about the universal law of the *'right use of power'*.

- **First form of leadership development**

This was the first form of leadership training and development. The process of activating the DNA to the 24th strand and accessing the original blueprint is therefore seen as a very holy and sacred process.

- **Wisdoms handed down**

These teachings, wisdoms, methods and skills have been handed down intact in an unbroken lineage, generation after generation, to the 'chosen ones'.

Now, this wisdom is made available and more accessible to the general public. These processes are continuing daily, with or without our awareness. There is truly nothing new under the sun.[58]

- ## Science, belief systems, and faith

At the same time, science has discovered that the ability to live in faith is partially heritable. Faith and/or belief systems, are hardwired into our genetic material

This led to the 'God gene hypothesis' that proposes that human beings inherit a set of genes that predispose them to believe in a higher power.

- ## The God Gene hypothesis

This idea was postulated by geneticist Dean Hamers, the director of the *Gene Structure and Regulation Unit at the U.S. National Cancer Institute.*

He wrote a book on the subject titled *The God gene: how faith is hardwired into our genes.* The God gene hypothesis is based on a combination of behavioural, genetic, neurobiological, and psychological studies.[59]

The major arguments of the theory are:

- Spirituality can be quantified by psychometric measurements.
- The underlying tendency to spirituality is partially heritable.
- Part of this heritability can be attributed to the gene VMAT2.
- This gene acts by altering *monoamine* levels.
- Spirituality arises in a population because spiritual individuals are favoured by natural selection.

However, over the years, various scientists and researchers, have been highly critical of this theory.

The fortunate result of this upheaval is that their criticisms have drawn attention to the idea of a connection between genes, heredity, and spirituality.

The truth is, the consequences of these findings have far-reaching implications for all and cannot be ignored.

Hereditary

Biological heredity and biological families are now making way for spiritual heredity and a new spiritual family.

Lifelong struggles with not fitting in with your biological family now make way for a re-identification with a new spiritual family with a new spiritual DNA that goes far beyond traditional teachings and biological genes.

This also includes a reinterpretation of the LGT[60] community from a genetic level.

- **Born again**

The challenge is to be 'reborn' or reconnected to become 'spiritual heirs'. We need to heal mind-virus and reconnect the 'broken mind' with the universal web – the higher spiritul mind.

- **Widespread implications**

These spiritual teachings have wide scientific implications as well. With the identification of a 'God gene', religion, science, psychology and spirituality will start to come together in order to provide deeper answers to the questions about authentic living and leading.

- **Authentic leaders**

At the same time, new authentic leaders, with a *New Leadership DNA*[61], are emerging. These are the leaders who will safely show the way into the future. One of the most important challenges of our generation is to identify and develop the 'leadership mind'.

This is the responsibility of everyone and not just a select few. Only then can we be confident to remain on the right path of a fulfilling, enlightened life, here and now.

The question is: What is the path back to authentic success and mindful living?

Understanding the path back

Once you are caught in the corrupt web of the illusion of the lie, you get disconnected from your authentic self, your DNA is disconnected on various levels and self-destruction is inevitable. You then revert to lower-order information and frequencies and the people who identify with these dark lies.

There are however a few things we need to take into consideration on our path back

- **Wake up and become free**

People who share the same version of the lie form groups who want to make you part of their 'family of darkness and despair'.

You can join one of these groups and remain here forever or – you could awake from this dark and depressing illusion, choose to reclaim your power, and to heal yourself from this unwelcome invader, the lie – the corrupter.

You also need to break free from the stronghold of outworn ideologies, dogmas, ideas, and let go of the people and groups who want to enslave you with their ideologies

- **Get connected**

You can choose to reconnect to the universal web, the higher mind, and use your inherent Power Intelligence.[62]

Power Intelligence is the conscious ability of managing and mastering personal and collective power to the benefit of all.[63] Power Intelligence is the way you activate your DNA success-blueprint.

You then become free, feel free and you are free to live your authentic self.

- **Stop self-destructive patterns**

Once you have woken up and become conscious of this destructive downward spiral, you choose to stop, turn around and head back home. You move to a new level of consciousness and embark on a new path of life and abundance. You ignite a whole new process and invest your time energy and money in growing in truth – freedom – love and compassion – light – Christ consciousness – sanity – the 'right mind'.

- **Become sensitive to those around you**

All corruption in any form and any place arises from the infection by the mind-virus. All corrupt persons, teams, organizations, governments, and even countries as a whole, are consciously and/or unconsciously infected with this mind-virus – the lie.

Very few people, teams, groups, political parties, or organizations, are however brave enough to admit their mental health and mind-virus status and seek help.

Corruption, the lie, then comes in many forms and with many faces. We find it in dishonest exploitation of power for personal gain and dishonest or illegal behavior by officials or people in positions of power, especially when they accept money in exchange for favors.

- ## Identify dysfunctional people and systems

This means most people with self-serving, ego-driven motives and intentions, are in essence corrupt and infected with the mind-virus.

Most people are currently vulnerable and living senseless even 'insane' lives. It is from this insanity and 'infection' we need to heal. We need to reclaim our power and put it to the right use, in our lives. If not, abuse or 'absence-of-use' is inevitable.

A self-destructive life becomes inevitable. Herein lies the choice to become power intelligent. Once again, we need to pay attention to mind-wellness.

- ## Stay objective – become the spectator

Once you can be objective and assess if you are disconnected or 'infected', as we do in order to attain our biological HIV-AIDS/Covis-19 status, you can begin with healing the broken connections.

You can then identify with a new group who shares your 'right mind' of truth and who too function on the frequency of light, love, and freedom.

You develop a whole new spiritual family with a whole new DNA.

- ## Become a catalyst

At the same time, you become aware of other people and groups who are infected with the mind-virus and render your services. You open your heart, mind, soul, and spirit and bring compassion, help and assistance to others.

You correct the corrupt program of ego- driven self-service. You change it to value- or soul-driven service and authentic success and quality living. You develop new leadership DNA and become a light bearer, pathfinder, and mapmaker.

You join hands with other like-minded ones and together we heal the body of light and find our way home.

- **Become a new generation freedom fighter**

It is from the mind-virus we need to free ourselves.[64] We need to heal the mind and take back our sanity. We were created to heal from a self-serving corrupt lifestyle and place our authentic self in a functional service that will benefit all. We can heal the body of light – the Christ consciousness or 'right mind'.[65]

You choose to return to your authentic, real-me, higher self and live an authentic life of compassion, love, abundance, fulfillment, and success. You consciously take back your power in body, mind, soul, and spirit.

You reconnect to your original blueprint, your authentic higher self. You 'fall in love' with your authentic self, your fellow human beings, with life on earth, with creation, the creator – God.

- **Climb the ladder of authentic success**

You embark on the journey back home. You heal your disconnections, and you climb the success ladder of real success by making your mark. You reconnect your DNA and take back the ability to co-create miracles with Source.

 You gain access to the storeroom of the universe. You change the 'hellish' lifestyle for – 'heaven on earth'.

You become an alchemist who can change lower order living in to higher-order experiences. You become a miracle-maker.

- **Become the Theoplexus**

You become aware of the *Theoplexus* and you consciously choose to become the *Theoplexus* – the place that Love, compassion, honesty, truth, and integrity meet all.[66]

You live your new life in compassion, love, abundance, and in service of the Greater Good, God - or whatever name you choose to depict a higher, universal power.

- **Make your mark**

Everyone has a contribution to make because everyone has a unique part to play in the tapestry of life. Everyone is therefore called to make their mark as only they can.

Things you can do

Here are a few things you can take into consideration to bring about the changes we want and need. This needn't take a lifetime if everyone is sensitised, make the right decisions, and take the right actions.

- **Your personal To-Do list**

Here are a few steps you can include I your self-development program:

> ➤ Do stocktaking of your life and assessment of your self

> ➤ Become conscious and aware of your own programs that are at default. Identify corrupt, erroneous values, wrong thinking, feelings, and destructive emotions. Change as necessary.

> ➤ Challenge outworn values, programs and thought

patterns and replace with new correct information

➢ Get a coach and/or mentor to help and assist you with change and transformation.

➢ Learn to distinguish between your ego-self and your authentic self or soul-self.

➢ Invest in self-mastery and self-development programs; read new books on healing DNA; attend workshops; identify and process the new and correct information

➢ Contact us for a personal coaching package by sending an email to info@powerintelligence.net tiled: request for coaching sessions.

➢ Invest in your authentic-self development, by reading new literature, attending lectures, and doing courses presented by leading authorities in the field of authentic living, and leading.

- **To-Do list: For authentic leaders**

Here are a few suggestions for those of you in leadership and/or influential positions

➢ As a leader, pathfinder, and mapmaker, you need to understand that the old ways of thinking and doing are not necessarily wrong – they are just old and worn out. When the season changes, so do mindsets and thinking change.

➢ Accept that a quantum leap is taking place. Some will be able to make this leap while others will stay behind.

➢ Keep what is still relevant in the new season while letting go of these old ways of thinking, old leadership training and ideas, outworn methods of doing business, financial management, and strategic planning.

> Be open and willing to embrace something new – become a ground-breaker

> Make sure that your group, company, organisation, team, and/or family, are sensitised to corruption as a mental health issue and the result of a mind-virus. Develop new HR-programs, skills and tools.

> Read the book *New Leadership DNA –developing enlightened leaders*[67]

> Change your leadership style by using the following guidelines below.

- **Changing your leadership style**

Here are the changes we can expect in leadership style

> Leaders having the power over people – now changing to – leaders releasing power within people (empowerment).

> Leaders seeing authority as domination – now changing to – leaders taking personal responsibility, taking dominion.

> Leaders maintaining their exclusive positions – now changing to – leaders upholding inclusive positions that benefit all people.

> Leaders finding power in numbers – now changing to – leaders acknowledging the power within people (number of powers). Developing number of powers

> Leaders defining success as 'acquiring positions

and possessions' – now changing to – leaders defining success as 'the quality of people we are becoming in the process of creating quality living that benefits all people'.

➢ Leaders promising to provide for the people – now changing to – assisting people to become self-sufficient

➢ Leaders leading from the tribal/collective mind – now changing to leaders leading from the quantum/universal mind.

➢ Choose to be a bold and courageous leader and way-shower

➢ Choose to be a fearless ground-breaker for a new season of quality living that includes success and progress for everyone.

➢ Bring your best self – your authentic self to the fabric of life.

Summary

The hope is that if you have read up and till here, you will have some new food for thought and that positive change will be inevitable.

Make a summary of things to do and people to contact.

Start just where you are.

Use the short table below as guideline.

Take one step at a time.

Enrol for one of our courses below

Current changes in authentic living and leading taking place

Changing from	Changing to
Gaining power over people	Releasing power in people
Authority is domination	Authority is taking dominion
Maintaining exclusive self-serving positions	Inclusive position of power and service
Finding power in numbers	Developing number of powers
Seeing success as acquiring possessions and positions	Success is becoming a real, authentic fully functional person
Promises to provide for people	Assisting people to become self-sufficient
Leading from the tribal mind	Leading from the quantum mind
Disconnected on a DNA level	Connected on a universal DNA level
Corruption and dishonesty in different forms	Truth, honesty and integrity as guiding values
Shadow ego-driven	Guided by real-me authentic self

oooOooo

INDEX

GLOSSARY

Affluence: Means 'full flow' and refers to material, physical, emotional, mental, psychological, spiritual and financial flow as the foundation of health and abundance.

Authentic: Having an undisputed origin; genuine; worthy of trust; reliance or belief. Authentic is Truth.

Authority: From Latin, *'auctōritās' and 'auctor'* meaning: *'author', 'the ability to create, grow, increase'* and *'he who obtains divine favor, increase' and 'auge' meaning 'to shine'. A person or group invested* with power; invested with the right or power to write and enforce rules or give orders; somebody or something with official power.

Calling: To request or order someone to do something; A claim on a person's time or life; Available whenever summoned to a particular pursuit or career; A strong urge to follow a particular career or do a particular type of work; to invoke as from heaven; To call, designate, summon, name, invoke and bring forth action.

Coaching: Training in how to deal with life, work, problems and interpersonal relationships.

Compassionate: Sympathetic, empathetic, kind, caring: Showing feelings of sympathy for the suffering of others, often with a desire to help.

Corrupt: All incorrect, shady, false, fraudulent information or; As verb: to make undesirable changes in meaning or introduce other errors into a text during copying; to introduce unintentional errors into computer data or software, making it unusable or unreliable; to become immoral or depraved, or cause somebody to become immoral or depraved; immoral or dishonest, especially as shown by the exploitation of a position of power or trust for personal gain.

Cure: To restore a sick person or animal to health; to bring to an end to an illness, disease or injury; treat illness successfully; restoring to full functionality.

COVID-19 virus: There are many different coronaviruses identified in animals but only a small number of these can cause disease in humans. On 7 January 2020, 'Severe Acute Respiratory Syndrome **Coronavirus** 2' (SARS-CoV-2) was confirmed as the causative agent of '**Coronavirus** Disease 2019' or **COVID-19**.

Dysfunctional: not fulfilling authentic function; failure

Energy: Vigour or power in action. Vitality and intensity of expression. Power exercised with vigour and determination. The capacity for action or accomplishment. From Greek: energies. Coined by Aristotle from energĕs (-en meaning 'at' and ergon meaning 'work'). Active-at-work. See 'power'.

Epidemic: An outbreak of a disease that spreads more quickly and more extensively among a group of people than would normally be expected. See: pandemic.

Epigenetics: Epigenetics is the study of the influence of the environment on the functioning of our genetic material or DNA.

It also includes the influence of our genetic functioning on the environment.

Evolve: To develop something gradually, often into something more complex or advanced, or undergo such development.

Fear: A chance or likelihood of an undesirable thing happening; an unpleasant feeling of anxiety or apprehension caused by the presence or anticipation of danger; an idea, thought, or other entity that causes feelings of fear; trepidation; anxiety.

Feelings: The sensation felt on touching something; the ability to perceive physical sensation in a part of the body; a perceived physical or mental sensation; and unqualified emotion.

Functional: Having a practical application, or serving a useful purpose: Useful, practical, well-designed, purposeful, being of service. (See useless).

Genetic barcoding: Hebert is a molecular biologist and director of the new Biodiversity Institute of Ontario at the University of Guelph in Canada. He is best known for his discovery and proliferation of DNA barcoding, which uses a specific section of genetic code to identify any species.

Happiness: Emotional fulfilment; includes contentment, being pleased, high spirits, exuberant; joyful; bliss, ecstasy.

HIV/AIDS: From: Human immunodeficiency virus (HIV) and Acquired immune deficiency syndrome or acquired immunodeficiency syndrome (AIDS).

Homo sapiens: *Homo* is Latin for 'human'. The word 'human' itself is from Latin *humanus*, an adjective cognate to homo, both thought to derive from a Proto-Indo-European word for "earth". 'Sapiens' is derived from '*sapience*' referring to 'wise man' or 'knowing man'. 'Sapience' is often defined as wisdom, or the ability of an organism or entity to act with appropriate judgment, a mental faculty which is a component of intelligence or alternatively may be considered an additional faculty, apart from intelligence, with its own properties.

Illusion: An erroneous perception of reality. An erroneous concept or belief.

Infectious: Caused by bacteria or viruses or other micro-organisms. Agents that are communicable, catching, transferable, transmittable and contagious. Agents capable of affecting the emotions and attitudes of others.

Influence: The effect of something on a person, thing, or event; the power that somebody has to affect other people's thinking or actions by means of argument, example, or force of personality.

Insanity: Extreme foolishness, or an act that demonstrates such foolishness. Mental illness, madness, lunacy. Informal: very stupid or crazy behavior that can cause serious problems, harm, or injury to others.

Inspiration: Stimulation of the faculties to a high level of feeling or activity. Theology: Divine guidance or influence exerted directly upon the mind and soul of man. The act of breathing in - inhalation. From: in-spiritus.

Inspire: To affect, guide or arouse by divine influence. To inhale; to breathe life into; to rouse latent energies, ideas or reverence; to enliven.

Integrity: From Latin 'integritãs' or 'intege', and is defined as "any intact unity or entity, whole, complete, perfect, virtuous".

Intelligence: From *intel* meaning 'between two' and *ligence* meaning 'to choose'. The human being is endowed with intelligence - the freedom to choose or 'free will'. According to Wechsler, *"intelligence is the aggregate or global capacity of the individual to act purposefully, to think rationally, and to deal effectively with his environment."*

Junk DNA and junk genes: Junk DNA and junk genes are provisional labels for the genes and portions of DNA sequence of a chromosome or a genome, for which no specific function can be identified. Many cellular biologists state that the so-called 'junk DNA', may turn out to be just as important as our much sought-after genes. Current studies of junk DNA are opening up unexplored areas of medical science and technology.

Leader: Comes from word leidð meaning: to show the way by going in advance; to guide by taking by the hand; escort; direct; to go first as a guide; to be at the head of; to act as director or commander; Somebody who guides or directs others; somebody or something in front of all others.

Leadership: Management, guidance, control, direction; the ability to guide, direct, or influence people; the office or position of the head of a body of people.

Light Body: Comes from 'chromosome'; chromo meaning 'light' and soma meaning body. We have 'light bodies' that surround our physical bodies and are connected to and controlled by our chromosomes. 'Light bodies' act as filters and attraction forces that attract everything in the proximity that resonates on the same frequency. As the chromosomes of our

DNA become reconnected and activated, they light up and emit a new light in our light bodies. When we are disconnected our levels of light are at a low and we attract dark forces. Also defined as the 'aura', 'spiritual body' or 'reticular-activating-system', the RAS.

Maturity: From Latin *'mature'*. Refers to becoming an evolving towards full development. It is a state or quality of being, of ripening, to complete and finish in natural growth and development. Maturity is becoming who you truly are and meeting the challenges of life. It is a level of full development for that time.

Mental health problems. Having a psychiatric disorder. An offensive term meaning extremely unintelligent or silly.

Mental health: Psychologically and mentally healthy. Mental health describes a level of psychological well-being, or an absence of a mental disorder. From the perspective of 'positive psychology' or 'holism', mental health may include an individual's ability to enjoy life, and create a balance between life activities and efforts to achieve psychological resilience. Mental health can also be defined as an expression of emotions, and as signifying a successful adaptation to a range of demands.

Mentor (verb): to mentor/mentoring: The personal name *Mentor* has been adopted in English as a term meaning 'someone who imparts wisdom to and shares knowledge with a less experienced colleague'.

Mentor: A person in Greek mythology; Friend of King Odyseus who mentored Odyseus's son Tellemachus in the ways and wisdoms of the world. Mentor prepared Tellemachus as king to take over the rule of his father when the time came.

Mind wellness. The desire or intention to act or behave in a particular way. A pattern of thinking or feeling characteristic of a particular group. See Mental health.

Mindful living: Actively attentive, or deliberately keeping something in mind. Conscious.

Miracle: An event that appears unexplained by the laws of nature, and so is held to be supernatural in origin, or 'an act of God'. The original word comes from *mirus* meaning 'causing one to smile', and at the same time it refers to 'mirror' or an occurrence that mirrors something/someone else. The words and phrases 'out of nowhere', coincidence, 'just thinking of', serendipity, and synchronicities, also denote 'miracles' [see wonder].

Mission: A special task given to a person or group to carry out; An aim or task that somebody believes it is his or her duty to carry out or to which he or she attaches special importance and devotes special care. A group of people sent to a country to represent their government, a business, or other organization.

Pandemic: A disease or condition that is found in a large part of a population. See: epidemic.

Potential: Possible but not yet realized; capable of being but not yet in existence; latent. The inherent ability or capacity for growth, development or coming into being or existence. 'Power-on-hold'.

Power: The ability or capacity to act or perform effectively. Strength or force to exercise control. The rate at which work is done. Used in an interrelated way with 'energy'.

Power Intelligence: The conscious ability to manage and master personal and collective power/energy and potential to the benefit of all.

Resilience: The ability to recover quickly from setbacks.

Quantum: A unit of light

Quantum leadership: Enlightened leadership originating in the quantum mind. Guidance and direction from a higher, universal connections.

Quantum mind: Frontal lobe functioning. Connecting with the quantum universe through the quantum mind/higher mind,

Sanity: The condition of being mentally healthy and able to make rational decisions. Includes wisdom, reason, understanding, common sense, common sense, reasonableness, and predictability.

Sapience: Used to define consciousness, wisdom, or the ability of an organism or entity to act with appropriate judgment, a mental faculty which is a component of intelligence; Alternatively it may be considered an additional faculty, apart from intelligence, with its own properties. See: *Homo sapience* (Homo – meaning only/one)

Source: From Latin '*surgere*' meaning to 'rise up' and 'to surge'. The place, person, or thing through which something has come into being or from which it has been obtained; a person, organization, book, or other text that supplies information or evidence; someone that causes , creates, or initiates something; a maker, A book, or other record, supplying primary or firsthand information, origin.

Theoplexus: Theoplex, Theo-plexus: A term denoting the place within and without, where Light-loves meets physicality and everything comes together. The 'healing of the body of Light'; takes place in the Theoplexus—a sacred place within all of us. .

Transcendence: To pass beyond (a human) limit; to exist above and independent of material experience or the universe; to rise above or across; to exceed; surpassing others of the same kind.

Transcendence: To pass beyond (a human) limit; to exist, above and independent of (material experience or the universe); to rise above or across; to exceed; surpassing others of the same kind.

Transcendent: Above and beyond material reality; referring to a deity.

Transformation: To change markedly the form or appearance; (transfiguration: to transform the figure or appearance).

Transmutation: To change from one form, nature, substance or state into another.

Useless: Not able to function properly. Loss of initial use.

Value: From the Latin word 'valere', that means "to be strong" or "to be valid". A value indicates the importance, validity, force or strength of something.

Vision: Defined as "a way to see, inner perception, imaginary insight", unusual competence in discernment or perception, intelligent foresight, mental images produced by the imagination, seeing as if with the eye of the supernatural.

Vulnerable: In a weak position, unable to resist illness, debility, or failure, open to harm, easily persuadable or liable to give in to temptation, powerless, exposed, helpless, defenceless, in danger, at risk, unable to resist illness, debilitation, or failure.

Wellbeing: Also wellness. A good, healthy, or comfortable state.

Wellness: Physical wellbeing, especially when maintained or achieved through good diet and regular exercise.

Whole brain emulation. (mind uploading): Sometimes called 'mind transfer', is the hypothetical process of transferring or copying a conscious mind from a brain to a non-biological substrate by scanning and mapping a biological brain in detail and copying its state into a computer system or another computational device.

oooOooo

WHO IS THE AUTHOR - DR BRENDA HATTINGH?

Dr. Brenda Hattingh is an international inspirational speaker, leadership coach and mentor and business, corporate and leadership consultant. Brenda invests her time in using personal and organisational power and success potential encoded as our unique DNA blueprint. This is a global first in personal and organisational training and development.

Brenda is committed to the development of a new level of consciousness with an awareness of the value of authentic living and leading. She focuses on assisting people, teams, companies and organisations – who are willing to bring their *best self* to the table.

As an author, Brenda brings to the table cutting edge information, books and training courses that include topics *like Power Intelligence – the intelligence of the future, New Success DNA*, and *New Leadership DNA*. She is Director of the *Power Intelligence Academy* and *The Academy for Authentic Leaders*. Brenda is also the *CEO of the Centre for Power Intelligence*

As an innovator, Brenda is committed to the development of a new generation of successful, innovative, inspired, thinkers and leaders. She speaks at events and conferences, presents workshops nationally and internationally, lectures at various universities and has published various books.

Her work is featured on TEDx Talks as Brenda introduces the next season of personal development and leadership training that includes tapping into your DNA-blueprint. Brenda is also the recipient of various awards including the *Professional Businesswoman of the Year Award*.

ENROLL FOR A PERSONAL 5-WEEK COURSE.

Title: LEARNING TO COACH YOURSELF TO ULTIMATE SUCCESS

This will be one of the best investments you have ever made.

Background

Times have changed and we need to think on our feet. You can only be super successful and flourish if you know how to coach yourself and manage your inner dialogue. Very few people, especially leaders, know how to do this.

At the moment, we are also experiencing a genetic migration. Humanity is going through a transformation, right down to a DNA level. This means we also need to learn how to activate our DNA success-blueprint. The information on how to do this is now available.

Contact us if you would first like to book a free session

What will you learn?

In this beginner course of *Learning to Coach Yourself*, that runs over five weeks, you will learn:

- Who your real-me is and what your personal purpose is
- How to tap into and activate your DNA success-blueprint
- How to master your inner dynamics and create affluence
- How to create the next level of success and happiness
- How to overcome inner blockages and pitfalls
- To understand the psychology of money and affluence
- To understand the science and psychology of real success
- How to become an authentic leader and influencer
- How to create health, wealth and happiness that benefits everyone
- And much more…

What will you receive:

- E-book 1. Coaching yourself to ultimate success. Who coaches who?
- E-book 2: Authentic living and leading. What is it and how to develop it
- Your personal workbook for your notes
- Five one-on-one personal coaching sessions via Skype, Zoom, or WhatsApp with Dr Brenda Hattingh.
- Three DNA-healing sessions
- A plan of action/map for the next season of your life.

Books will soon be available on www.amazon.com/books

Who should invest in this course?

Everyone who wants to move forward and create their best life. This includes people like you and me, leaders, teachers, parents, business-people, couples …

How to book your *Course. Learning to coach yourself?*

Send an email to: info@powerintelligence.net. We will send all the necessary information to your inbox.

See our website: http://www.brendahattingh.com

This course is also Avaible for teambuilding, and leadership development in companies and organisations.

oooOooo

Follow the series

Authentic Living and leading

- Book 1: The authentic self. Who am I?
- Book 2. Coaching your self to ultimate success
- Book 3: Authentic Leadership: Recovering your DNA leadership-blueprint
    - Book 4: Power Intelligence – The intelligence of the future
    - Book 5: DNA – Climbing the new ladder of success.
    - Book 6: The quantum leap to authenticity. Will you make it?

More books and courses in this series will be released later in 2021.

For books see: Amazon's Brenda Hattingh Page

Join our mailing list available here and get book one free

Get your free *Daily Power Tools for power People* delivered to your inbox here.

For courses see the Power Intelligence Leadership Academy here

OoooOooo

BOOK DR BRENDA HATTINGH AS SPEAKER

To book Dr Brenda Hattingh as an exciting, entertaining, and inspirational keynote speaker for your next event, or conference and training session, contact us by sending an email to:

Email: info@powerintelligence.net

See website: http://www.brendahattingh.com

ooo0ooo

BOOK DR BRENDA FOR LEADERSHIP TRAINING
Email us: info@powerintelligence.net

ooo0ooo

MORE BOOKS AND COURSES

For books see: Amazon's Brenda Hattingh Page

Or contact us: info@powerintelligence.net

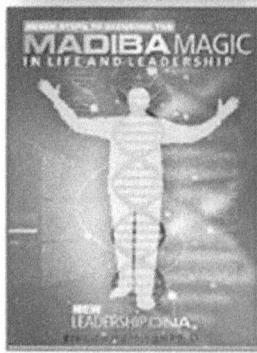

REFERENCES

[1] Hattingh, Brenda. (2016). *Curing Corruption. 7 Things you can do to solve the dilemma of our time.* Currency Communications: Johannesburg.

[2] See http://www.fin24.com/Economy/R700bn-lost-to-corruption-in-20-years-20150128 Statistics released by The Institute of Internal Auditors on Wednesday Jan 28 2015

[3] New jobs created at +/-ZAR 350 000/job. See: http://www.moneyweb.co.za/archive/why-does-it-cost-the-idc-so-much-to-create-one-job/

[4] See article: www.businesstech.co.za. *Advisory group puts date to South Africa's collapse.*

[5]. See article as above: www.businesstech.co.za

[6] Loss Management is a business practice that seeks to detect, identify, investigate and prevent events that cause a drop in value of any of an organization's revenues, assets and services. Loss- management improvements may involve changes in a business's operating policies and business model in order to limit instances of accidental and/or intentional loss.

[7] See website: www.vocabulary.com/dictionary/corruption

[8] See website: www.investopedia.com/terms/c/corruption.asp

[9] See website: http://www.corruptie.org/en/corruption/what-is-corruption/

[10] See website: http://www.corruptie.org/en/corruption/what-is-corruption/

[11] See: https://www.oecd.org/cleangovbiz/49693613.pdf

[12] The Heritage Illustrated Dictionary of the English Language. International Edition. Morris, William (Ed). American Heritage Publishing Co.Inc: New York.

[13] Hattingh, Brenda. (2012. b). *Power Intelligence. Mastering your miracle mind.* Currency Communications: Johannesburg.

[14] Hattingh, B. 2012 (a). *New Success DNA. What you should know and how to activate it.* Currency communications International: Johannes burg.

[15] See: https://www.oecd.org/cleangovbiz/49693613.pdf

[16] Mental health: https://www.google.com/search?q=definition+mental+health&oq=Definition+mental+health&aqs=chrome.0.0l8.16617j1j15&sourceid=chrome&ie=UTF-8

[17] Mental health disorders: https://www.psychiatry.org/patients-families/what-is-mental-illness

[18] Hattingh, B. 2012 (a). *New Success DNA. What you should know and how to activate it. Currency communications International: Johannesburg.*

[19] The Huma Genome Project: https://www.genome.gov/human-genome-project

[20] Hattingh, Brenda. (2020). *Coaching yourself to ultimate success. Who coaches who?* Currency Communications Pty.Ltd.: Johannesburg.

[21] See website: http://en.wikipedia.org/wiki/Soul

[22] Carl Jung used the term *principium individuationis*, or principle of *individuation*. This describes the manner in which a thing is identified from other things. See website: http://org/wiki/Individuation

[23] Planes of existence: In esoteric cosmology, *'a plane'*, other than the physical plane is conceived as a subtle state of consciousness that transcends the known physical universe. See website: http://en.wikipedia.org/wiki/Plane_(esotericism) See book: *Authentic self – expressing the real you.*

[24] See glossary: Planes.

[25] Light that is not visible to the naked eye. Comic light rays are rising according to NASA. See website: http://science.nasa.gov/science-news/science-atnasa/2009/29sep_cosmicrays/ See article in *Time magazine*: Website: http://www.time.com/time/magazine/article/0,9171,991839,00.html

[26] Hattingh, Brenda. (2012 b). *Power Intelligence. Mastering the Miracle Mind.* Currency Communications Pty.Ltd.: Johannesburg

[27] Hattingh, B. 2012 (a). *New Success DNA. What you should know and how to activate it. Currency communications International: Johannesburg.*

[28] Quantum leadership: Leaders who are connected to and understand the quantum mind and quantum guidance. Enlightened leaders (See glossary)

[29] Hattingh, Brenda. (2012 c). *New Leadership DNA. Developing enlightened leaders.* Currency Communications: Johannesburg. (See Chapter 21)

[30] See: *New Success DNA*. Chapter 10.

[31] Hattingh, Brenda. (2012 b*). Power Intelligence. Mastering your miracle mind.* Currency Communications Int: Johannesburg.

[32] Hattingh, Brenda. (2012 c). *New Leadership DNA. Developing enlightened leaders.* Currency Communications: Johannesburg.

[33] Hattingh, Brenda, (2016). *Curing Corruption. 7 Steps you can do to cure the epidemic of our time.* Currency Communications Int: Johannesburg.

[34] Koonin, EV. Senkevich, TG, Dolja, VV. 2006. The ancient virus world and evolution of cells. *Biol. Direct.* 2006;1:29.

[35] See: Hattingh, Brenda. (2020.a) *New success DNA. What you should know and how to develop it.* Currency Communications: Johannesburg.

[36] See: Wikipedia : http://en.wikipedia.org/wiki/Introduction_to_viruses.

[37] Although most of this information is on the internet in various forms, more scientific and technical information is accessible from other sources including Wikipedia:Viruses: http://en.wikipedia.org/wiki/viruses.

[38] HIV - human immunodeficiency virus (HIV) AIDS - 'Acquired immune deficiency syndrome' or 'acquired immuno-deficiency syndrome'.

[39] Hattingh, Brenda. (2020) *Authentic living and leading. What you should know and how to live it.* Currency Communication. Johannesburg.

[40] Insanity. Being of unsound mind
[41] Hattingh, Brenda. (2014). *Power Tools for Power People*. Currency Communications. Johannesburg.
[42] Useless – los of authentic use; dysfunctional.
[43] Lipton, B. 2008. *The biology of belief*. Hay House. CA.
[44] Epigenetics: See. https://www.cdc.gov/genomics/disease/epigenetics.htm
[45] Genetic barcoding. See: https://www.sciencedirect.com/topics/medicine-and-dentistry/dna-barcoding
[46] Hebert and barcoding: Hebert is a molecular biologist and director of the new Biodiversity Institute of Ontario at the University of Guelph in Canada
[47] See New Success DNA: Chapter 5.
[48] Nowak, R. 1994. Mining treasures from "junk DNA". *Science* 161: 529-540. See glossary: 'Junk genes'
[49] See Chapter 14: Emotional mastery
[50] See: New Success DNA
[51] Hattingh, B. (2014). *Power Tools for Power People*. Currency Communications: JHB.
[52] Hattingh, Brenda. (2012 c). *New Leadership DNA. Developing enlightened leaders*. Currency Communications: Johannesburg. (Chapter 21)
[53] Training in *Power Intelligence DNA Healing:* Commences Sept. 2016. For more details see website: www.brendahattingh.com.
[54] Power Intelligence Leadership Academy. https://power-intelligence-leadership-academy.teachable.com
Book: Coaching yourself to ultimate success. Avaible on Amazon.com
[55] See website: www.cancer.org
[56] Artificial intelligence: Artificial intelligence, is intelligence demonstrated by machines, unlike the natural intelligence. displayed by humans and animals.
[57] Nanotechnology is the use of matter on an atomic, molecular, and supramolecular scale for industrial purposes.
[58] See: The Rocky Mountain Mystery School (aka: Modern Mystery School). Website: http:www.RMMSint.com.
[59] Hamer, Dean. 2005. *The God gene: How faith is hardwired into our genes*. Amcor Publishers. New York.
[60] LGT community – lesbian, gay and transgender community
[61] Hattingh, B. 2012 (a). *New Success DNA. what you should know and how to activate it. Currency communications International: Johannes burg.*
Hattingh, B. 2012 (b). *Power Intelligence. Mastering your miracle mind.* Currency Communications: Johannesburg.
[62] Hattingh, Brenda. (2012 b). Power Intelligence. Mastering your miracle mind. Currency Communications Int: Johannesburg.
[63] Hattingh, Brenda. (2012 b). Power Intelligence. Mastering your miracle mind. Currency Communications Int: Johannesburg.
[64] Hattingh, B. 2012. *Life, stumbling block or stepping stone.* Currency Communications Int: Johannesburg. See chapters 9 & 10.
[65] Foundation for Inner Peace. 1996. A course in miracles. Penguin Books. New York.
[66] See: New Success DNA. (pp. 370-372)
[67] Hattingh, Brenda. (2012 c). *New Leadership DNA. Developing enlightened leaders*. Currency Communications: Johannesburg.

www.ingramcontent.com/pod-product-compliance
Lightning Source LLC
Chambersburg PA
CBHW070356220526
45467CB00001B/406